Fundamentals of Human Communication

COMM 1310
2018–2019 Guidebook

Texas State University
Department of Communication Studies

601 University Drive • San Marcos, TX 78666-4616
512.245.2165 • Fax 512.245.3138

http://www.commstudies.txstate.edu/
Member **THE TEXAS STATE UNIVERSITY SYSTEM™**

Excerpts taken from:

Communication: Principles for a Lifetime, Seventh Edition
by Steven A. Beebe, Susan J. Beebe, and Diana K. Ivy

Public Speaking: An Audience-Centered Approach, Tenth Edition
by Steven A. Beebe and Susan J. Beebe

Printed in the United States of America   1   18

000200010272099030

HG

www.pearsoned.com

ISBN 10:   0-135-21495-5
ISBN 13: 978-0-135-21495-4

Your Career Path Begins with Communication

TEXAS ★ STATE
COMMUNICATION
STUDIES
stars. rising.

Welcome to **COMM1310** | You have already enrolled in the first class toward becoming a Communication Studies major or minor.

WHAT CAN YOU DO WITH A MAJOR IN COMMUNICATION STUDIES?

Sales Director. Teacher. Elected Official. Fund Raiser. Event Manager. Speech Writer. Campaign Director. Lawyer. Public Information Officer. Management Analyst. Foreign Service Officer. Recreational Coordinator. Counselor. Author. Health Services Manager. Editor. Performer. Legislative Assistant. Executive Director. Interviewer. Negotiator. Labor Relations Specialist. Customer Service Manager. Researcher. Communication Consultant. Direct Hire Recruiter. Government Administrator. Instructional Program Designer. Sales Director. Marketing Communication Professional. College Admissions Counselor. Researcher. Director of a Nonprofit Organization. External Affairs Specialist. E-learning Program Developer. Public Relations Specialist. Corporate Trainer. Advertising Sales Director. Interactive Project Coordinator. E-learning Manager. Entrepreneur. International Market Research Professional. Press Secretary. Executive Management & Leadership. Private Investigator. Security Agent.

HERE ARE WHAT SOME OF OUR GRADUATES ARE DOING WITH THEIR **COMM STUDIES** MAJOR FROM TEXAS STATE UNIVERSITY-SAN MARCOS.

Meghan Butler, B.A. 2002
Vice President,
Dye, Van Mol & Lawrence Public Relations
& Advertising

Deidra Flynn Dobson, B.A. 2008
Instructor, American Sign Language
and Interpreter

Lindsey Mask, B.A. 1998
News Anchor/Reporter for an ABC Affiliate;
Press Secretary for Member of U.S.
Congress

Megan McChesney, B. A. 2008
Account Executive,
VMware, Virtualization

Justin Mick, B.A. 2005
Materials & Logistics Coordinator,
SeAH Steel Corp., USA

Brandy P. Priest, B.A. 2005
Marketing Consultant, Fox News/NBC
Television

Alison Teague, B. A. 2008
Account Executive, Direct Hire Recruiter,
Professional Alternatives

Matt Trietsch, B.A. 2008
Senior Human Resources and Training
Associate,
San Antonio College
Cloud Infrastructure Software

Brendan Radomski, B.A. 2008
Walter P. Moore Engineering

Stephanie Irwin, B. A. 2004
Briefing Analyst,
Executive Briefing Center Dell, Inc.

Marcie Leigh, B. A. 2006
Comptroller, PSW Homes
Sustainable Urban Homes

Clayton Medford, B.A. 2006
Communication Director,
The Chairman of the Board of Supervisors,
Fairfax County, Virginia
M.A. 2012; Hospital Sales
Specialist, Abbott Nutrition

Madeline Rich, B.A. 2015
Stewardship Coordinator,
Dell Children's Medical Center

WANT TO LEARN MORE ABOUT BEING A **COMM STUDIES** MAJOR?

Visit with your COMM 1310 Instructor to learn more about the many career options available to COMM Studies majors. Or visit us on the web at www.commstudies.txstate.edu.

Table of Contents

Module 1

Principles of Human Communication   1

Preparing for Exams in Comm 1310   49

Module 2

Communicating in the Interpersonal Context   59

Module 3

Communicating in the Informative Speaking Context   87

Module 4

Communicating in Small Group and Team Contexts   137

Course Description & General Objectives

Course Syllabus

According to the authors of your textbook, "human communication is the process of making sense out of the world and sharing that sense with others by creating meaning through the use of verbal and nonverbal messages" (Beebe, Beebe, & Ivy, 2019, p. 5). It is a process of not only perceiving and interpreting others' verbal and nonverbal messages, but also using these messages to stimulate appropriate meanings in the minds of others. This course teaches the principles that are fundamental for every aspect of human communication. In the course of our study of human communication we will discuss a myriad of skills, ideas, concepts, and contexts. The number of terms, ideas, skills, and competencies can be overwhelming. To help stitch together the barrage of ideas and information, we will organize our study around five principles. Together, these five principles provide a framework for our discussion of the importance and pervasiveness of human communication.

The Five Principles

1. Be aware of your communication with yourself and others.
2. Effectively use and interpret verbal messages.
3. Effectively use and interpret nonverbal messages.
4. Listen and respond thoughtfully to others.
5. Appropriately adapt messages to others.

Although the principles of human communication remain the same regardless of the context in which they occur, the context affects the preceding principles and the communication process in unique ways. In this course, we will examine and apply the five principles to three contexts including (1) Interpersonal, (2) Group/Team, and (3) Presentational Speaking. Our goal is to present both classic and contemporary research conclusions about the role and importance of communication in our lives.

Course Objectives and General Education Learning Outcomes

After completing COMM 1310, students should be able to:

- List, describe, and explain the five principles of human communication and identify how they are integrated into the interpersonal, group/team, and presentational speaking contexts.
- Analyze and appropriately manage interpersonal conflict by using the five principles of human communication.
- Identify and describe appropriate adaptive messages in intercultural communication situations and demonstrate appropriate affective responses to intercultural communication interactions.
- Develop, organize, and deliver an informative presentation integrating the five principles into your presentation.
- Develop, organize, and deliver a persuasive presentation integrating the five principles into your presentation.

COURSE TEXTBOOK AND GUIDEBOOK – BOTH REQUIRED

Beebe, S. A., Beebe, S. J., & Ivy, D. K. (2019). *Communication: Principles for a Lifetime* (7th ed.). Boston: Pearson Education. (Available at Bookstore – A La Carte text with binder and Online Access Code for Student Speeches)

Texas State University Department of Communication Studies. (2018–2019). *Fundamentals of Human Communication: COMM 1310 Guidebook.* Boston: Pearson Education. (Available at the University Bookstore)

Course Requirements   POINTS

1. Attendance (refer to policy below)	+/-
2. Pre-Post Tests	10
3. Three Examinations	
Exam #1	100
Exam #2	100
Exam #3	100
4. Written Assignment	
Diversity and Communication Assignment	30
5. Oral Presentations	
Informative Presentation	100
Outline, *Turnitin*, Audience Adaptation Plan	15
Speaking Notes	5
Persuasive Presentation	60
Outline, *Turnitin*, Audience Adaptation Plan	15
Speaking Notes	5
Problem-Solving Report	40
Group Member Assessment	20
Total Points	600

Grades will be distributed in the following manner:

537–600	A
477–536	B
417–476	C
357–416	D
000–356	F

Course Requirements Overview

Course Requirement Policy:
Course requirements **MUST be submitted on time (by the deadline communicated by your instructor) in order to be accepted**. Thus, we DO NOT accept late work. Any exceptions, determined on a case-by-case basis, will require extremely compelling, well-documented reasons. If you experience dire circumstances (e.g. accident, hospitalization, family death, etc.) you **MUST** provide documentation to your instructor **via notification by the Dean of Students office**.

Attendance:
Your attendance will be factored into the final grade. Because COMM 1310 emphasizes cognitive as well as experiential learning, it is important that you attend every class. A record of absences will be kept for each student. Attendance will be checked at the beginning and end of each class session. The Department of Communication Studies does not make the distinction between excused or unexcused absences. Generally, absences equal to the number of times a class meets in 1 week are without penalty. For example:

- Classes that meet three times each week (M/W/F), your first three absences are without penalty.
- Classes that meet two times each week (T/H), your first two absences are without penalty.
- Classes that meet one time each week (Evening Classes), your first absence is without penalty.

Your penalty-free absences are to be used as an insurance policy that will cover you during times of unforeseen emergency or illness.

Absences in excess of the specified number listed above will lower your final grade by 10 points for each day missing. For example, if you have a T/H class schedule, and miss 3 days, your final course grade will be lowered 10 points. In other words, a 537 (A) final course grade becomes a 527 (B). Students with excessive absences will be encouraged to drop the course since a passing grade will be difficult to attain. If you attain perfect attendance and your attendance remains punctual, 10 bonus points will be added to your final course grade. For example, a 527 (B) final course grade will become a 537 (A). Punctuality is defined as being less than 5 minutes late at the beginning of class and remaining until the class is officially dismissed.

Pre- and Post-Tests:
You will complete two online assessments in this course. These have been created to determine your knowledge of communication principles coming into and upon completion of the class. You will be assigned 10 points for completing BOTH online assessment instruments.

Written Assignment (Understanding Differences Assignment):
An important component of COMM 1310 is awareness and adaptation of others around us and how their diversity influences communication between us. To help you understand this, you will be expected to participate in a classroom activity that requires you to engage in a multicultural experience and then reflect on that experience. This written report of your experiential learning is worth 30 points. As a component of this assignment, you will need to upload your paper to the *Turnitin* Web site.

Examinations:
You will take three exams. Each of the exams is multiple-choice format and objective based. Study guide questions for each chapter are located throughout this Guidebook.

Answering these questions as you work through the chapters will prepare you for the exams. Each exam includes 50 multiple-choice items, with each item being worth 2 points. Please bring a No. 2 pencil to all examinations. We will provide the appropriate answer sheets.

Oral Presentations:

You will develop and deliver two oral presentations. The first presentation features an informative presentation, and the second features a persuasive, group problem-solving presentation. Assignments, evaluation criteria, and evaluation forms are located in the student Guidebook. You will have the opportunity to earn up to 5 points per presentation for visiting our Communication Lab in the Alkek Library. However, **if you schedule an appointment and fail to show up or cancel your appointment (at least 24 hours in advance), your presentation score will be reduced by 5 points.**

Course Policies

Late Work Policy:

We DO NOT accept late assignments. Any exceptions, determined on a case-by-case basis, will require extremely compelling, well-documented reasons. If you experience dire circumstances (e.g., accident, hospitalization, or family death) you MUST provide documentation via notification by the Dean of Students office.

Policy on Academic Honesty:

Learning and teaching take place best in an atmosphere of intellectual freedom and openness. All members of the academic community are responsible for supporting freedom and openness through rigorous personal standards of honesty and fairness. Plagiarism and other forms of academic dishonesty undermine the very purpose of the university and diminish the value of an education. All graded work—examination answers, oral presentation outlines, and oral presentations—must be the original work of the student claiming credit for it. Outlines for both the informative and group presentations will be checked through the *Turnitin* database. An *"Originality Report"* will be submitted with outlines. Students guilty of knowingly using or attempting to use another person's work as though it were their own, and students guilty of knowingly permitting or attempting to permit another student to use their work will receive a grade of F for COMM 1310. Students who are uncertain regarding what actions constitute plagiarism in COMM 1310 should consult the instructor.
http://www.txstate.edu/effective/upps/upps-07-10-01.html

Special Circumstances:

Students with special needs (as documented by the Office of Disability Services) should identify themselves at the beginning of the semester to their respective instructor.

Research Participation:

In some classes you may be asked to participate in faculty and graduate student research projects and various course assessment studies. The Department of Communication Studies and appropriate University reviewing agencies will have approved such research projects in advance. We thank you in advance for your voluntary participation in these research projects.

Policy on Fairness:

Texas State is committed to social justice. We concur with that commitment and expect to maintain a positive learning environment based upon open communication, mutual respect, and nondiscrimination. Texas State does not discriminate on the basis of race, color, national origin, age, sexual orientation, religion, or disability. Any suggestions as to how to further such a positive and open environment in this course will be appreciated and given serious consideration.

Policy on Classroom Civility:

Students are full partners in fostering a classroom environment that is conducive to learning. In order to assure that all students have the opportunity to gain from time spent in class, unless otherwise approved by the instructor, students are prohibited from engaging in any form of behavior that detracts from the learning experience of fellow students. Inappropriate behavior in the classroom may result in a request for the offending student to leave class.

Classroom Misconduct:

Classroom misconduct may be classified as behavior that disturbs the teaching function, the students, or the instructor during the class period.

Examples of Classroom Misconduct: Activated cellular phones, inappropriate challenges to authority, demands for special treatment, frequent episodes of leaving and then returning to class, eating or drinking in the classroom, excessive tardiness, leaving lecture/lab early, making offensive remarks, missing deadlines, prolonged chattering, reading newspapers during class, sleeping, arriving late to class, dominating discussions, shuffling backpacks or notebooks, using laptops or any unrelated materials, and overt inattentiveness are examples of inappropriate classroom behavior.

Extra Credit:

Although COMM 1310 does not have an official policy on administering extra credit, most instructors offer extra credit in a conservative manner using the following guidelines:

- Maximum of 10 points
- Extra credit is defined as course-appropriate engagement activities that occur outside of class.
- You will have the opportunity to earn up to 5 points per presentation for visiting the Communication Lab in the Alkek Library to receive feedback on your presentation prior to your speech day. However, **if you fail to show up to your appointment and do not cancel your appointment online (at least 24 hours before your appointment time), you will receive a 5-point deduction on your oral presentation score.**

Communicating with Your Instructor

Using E-mail Effectively

Like a letter or an English essay, an effective e-mail is composed of parts.

Subject Line.   This should be clear and meaningful.

Greeting.   This should address the recipient by name or title and name (e.g., Dear Professor Claus or Smith).

Small Talk.   Just as you would make small talk in a conversation, you should in an e-mail as well. It serves to break the ice, and can also establish a relationship (e.g., I enjoyed class today and thought the topic was very interesting, *or*, I see your Spurs won last night. Did you enjoy the game? or, I don't know if you remember me, but we met at the NCA conference and you offered to help me with my project).

Body.   Just as with a speech or a paper, the body is the meat and potatoes of your message. Your major ideas go here.

Closing. Show your appreciation or sincerity, and give your name (e.g., Thank you, Susie Q. or Sincerely, Johnnie).

- **Things to Remember.** Even if you do everything above, your e-mails can still be ineffective if you neglect these basics:
- **Proofread!** Spell-check is a must, but remember that it can miss homonyms and other mistakes.
- **Use Paragraphs!** Nothing is uglier on the screen, and nothing is harder to decipher, than one undifferentiated hunk of text. It is not necessary to indent, but do double-space between paragraphs. And remember, one idea per paragraph, just like in English class.
- **Use Bullets!** If you have multiple ideas or questions, a bulleted format is very effective.
- **KISS!** Keep it simple, silly! If your e-mail is long and rambling, it will not get read. Keep your message short and to the point.

MODULE 1
PRINCIPLES OF HUMAN COMMUNICATION

After completing this module (Chapters 1-6), you will be able to:

PRINCIPLE 1
Be aware of your communication with yourself and others.

- Identify three different models of human communication (active, interactive, and transactive) and explain how these models reflect your own communication and the communication you have with others.
- Explain the power and importance of symbols in human communication.
- Describe the role and function of perception in the communication process.
- Recognize common perceptual errors and identify ways to enhance the perception process: perception checking and empathy.
- Understand the role self-concept plays in influencing communication with self and others.
- Understand the role self-esteem plays in influencing communication with self and others.

PRINCIPLE 2
Effectively use and interpret verbal messages.

- Identify and avoid language that impedes effective communication: abstract language, biased language, evaluative language, controlling messages, manipulative messages, detached messages, rigid messages, superior messages, and defensive communication such as gunnysacking.
- Identify and use strategies to enhance verbal quality, clarity, and accuracy.

PRINCIPLE 3
Effectively use and interpret nonverbal messages.

- Differentiate between verbal and nonverbal messages.
- Explain functions of nonverbal messages: repeating, substituting, complementing, accenting, regulating, and contradicting.
- Identify and discriminate between various types of nonverbal messages: appearance, kinesics, eye contact, facial expressions, vocalics, haptics, proxemics, territoriality, and environment.
- Identify and explain three primary dimensions used for interpreting nonverbal communication accurately: immediacy, arousal, and dominance.

PRINCIPLE 4
Listen and respond thoughtfully to others.

- Understand the importance of accurately listening to others.
- Identify barriers to effective listening.
- Differentiate between informational, critical, analytical, and empathic forms of listening.
- Identify and use strategies to enhance informational, critical, analytical, and empathic forms of listening.
- Seek and appropriately respond to corrective feedback to enhance communication.

PRINCIPLE 5
Appropriately adapt messages to others.

- Recognize and appreciate the influence of culture and gender on communication behavior.
- Identify cultural differences in communication and identify and use strategies to adapt to those differences.
- Identify gender-based differences in communication and identify and use strategies to adapt to those differences.

Chapter 1
Lecture Notes

Exam 1

Communication Cometence - define
Know identity's -
Know different selfs
Know communication models & Processes
   Ch 1-3 look @ models
  Know diff between self esteem & self concept
  Ch2 - Perception Process
  6 methods for using words to estabish relation
ships
verbal { guny sacing
   { communication barriers
Ch 4
   Pg 84 diagram
   functions of nonverbal comm - compliment
  Know barriers to listening
  *Stages of listening
  *Styles of listening
  Ch 6 - All

Chapter 2
Lecture Notes

Chapter 3
Lecture Notes

Chapter 4
Lecture Notes

Chapter 5
Lecture Notes

Chapter 6
Lecture Notes

Principle 5 · Adapt
  Assuming Superiority - better than (Texas)
  Stereotyping - frequent
  Prejudice - Act on Stereotypes

Chapter 1 Why Study Communication?

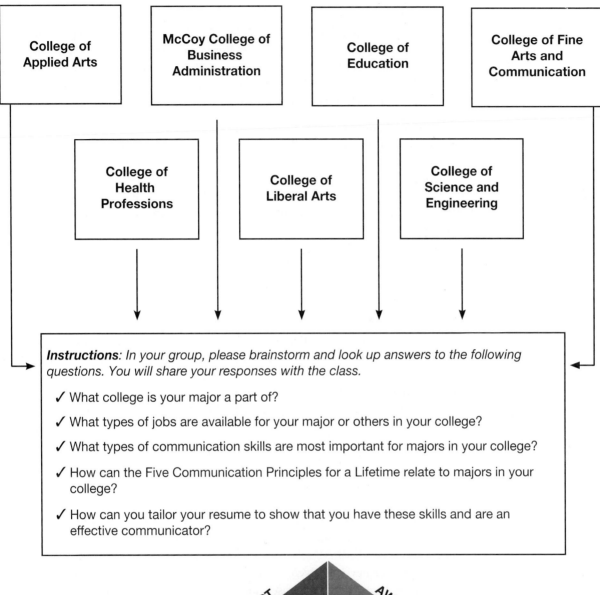

| College of Applied Arts | McCoy College of Business Administration | College of Education | College of Fine Arts and Communication |

| College of Health Professions | College of Liberal Arts | College of Science and Engineering |

Instructions: *In your group, please brainstorm and look up answers to the following questions. You will share your responses with the class.*

✓ What college is your major a part of?

✓ What types of jobs are available for your major or others in your college?

✓ What types of communication skills are most important for majors in your college?

✓ How can the Five Communication Principles for a Lifetime relate to majors in your college?

✓ How can you tailor your resume to show that you have these skills and are an effective communicator?

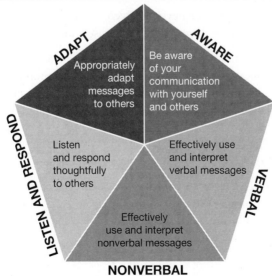

ADAPT — Appropriately adapt messages to others

AWARE — Be aware of your communication with yourself and others

Effectively use and interpret verbal messages

Listen and respond thoughtfully to others

Effectively use and interpret nonverbal messages

LISTEN AND RESPOND

VERBAL

NONVERBAL

SOURCE: Communication: Principles for a Lifetime, 7/e Steven A. Beebe 0134553527

What do professionals say about communication skills?

Engineering and management schools are not doing enough to prepare students, according to a number of recent studies, but the failure is not happening where one might expect it. "Universities generally do a pretty good job when it comes to teaching *hard* skills. . .But they don't do so well with the *softer* competencies, including communications, teamwork and systemic thinking."

Wladawsky-Berger, I. (2014, December 28). Preparing students for an increasingly complex business world. *Wall Street Journal*. Retrieved from http://blogs.wsj. com/cio/2014/12/28/preparing-students-for-an-increasingly-complex-business-world/

"What I'm looking for are listening skills. Do they listen and hear me? Do they have the ability to modulate behavior based on the specific question I ask and are they able to talk with a level of abstraction about who they are? I've probably learned 70 percent of what I'm going to learn about somebody in [that] first interaction."

Fernandez, P. (2014, July 18). Yes, I'm direct. But you should be, too. Interview by A. Bryant. *The New York Times*, p. B2.

"In many ways Communication Studies is the right offering at the right time. The discipline is extremely well positioned as the digital economy, social networking and the move toward media creation rises to prominence. Concepts that may have been more abstract for students fifteen years ago such as relationship networks, group communication, and media theory are becoming vitally relevant knowledge that a wide ranging student body want to obtain."

Schmitt, J. (2014, October 22). Communication studies rises to relevance. *Huffington Post*. Retrieved from http://www.huffingtonpost.com/jason-schmitt/communication-studies-ris_b_6025038.html

"The study of writing and analyses of texts equip science students to communicate their findings as professionals in the field. . . .Scientists are often unable to communicate effectively because, as Cornell University president David J. Skorton points out, 'many of us never received the education in the humanities or social sciences that would allow us to explain to nonscientists what we do and why it is important.'"

Jackson-Hayes, L. (2015, February 18). We don't need more STEM majors. We need more STEM majors with liberal arts training. *The Washington Post*. Retrieved from http://www.washingtonpost.com/posteverything/wp/2015/02/18/we-dont-need-more-stem-majors-we- need-more-stem-majors-with-liberal-arts-training/

"The ability to communicate effectively is the single most important skill kids need to succeed in life, say the nation's grown-ups."

Stevens, H. (2015, February 24). Kids need communication skills above all, survey says. Chicago Tribune. Retrieved from http://www.chicagotribune.com/lifestyles/ct-skills-adults-think-kids-need-balancing-20150224-column.html

Chapter 1: Myths about Human Communication

Respond to the following statements as true or false.

_____ 1. Good communicators are born, not made.

_____ 2. The more you communicate, the better your communication will be.

_____ 3. Unlike effective speaking, effective listening really cannot be taught.

_____ 4. Opening lines such as "how are you?" or "fine weather today" serve no useful communication purpose.

_____ 5. The best way to communicate with someone from a different culture is exactly as you would with someone from your own culture.

_____ 6. When verbal and nonverbal messages contradict each other, people believe the verbal message.

_____ 7. Complete openness should be the goal of any meaningful interpersonal relationship.

_____ 8. Interpersonal conflict is a sign that your relationship is in trouble.

_____ 9. Like good communicators, leaders are born, not made.

_____ 10. Fear of public speaking is detrimental and an effective speaker must learn to eliminate it.

Principle 1:   Perception Checking

Purpose

To check your initial perceptions of other individuals and to understand how perceptions are formed.

Instructions

Without discussing the exercise with your partner, complete the following items based on what you think is most likely for your partner. When you are finished, check your perceptions of each other. Discuss with your partner ways to enhance the perceptual accuracy of your perceptions. (Refer to textbook, **Chapter 2.**)

1. Most likely to watch:

____ A romantic comedy

____ An action film

____ A horror movie

✓ A comedy

____ A documentary

____ A foreign film

3. Most likely to listen to:

✓ Rap/Hip Hop Music

____ Classical Music

____ Country Music

____ Pop Music

____ Rock/Metal

5. Most likely to look for in a partner:

____ Intelligence

____ Looks

✓ Personality

____ Money

____ Sense of humor

____ Spirituality

7. Most likely to watch:

____ Sitcoms

____ News shows

✓ TV drama

____ Sports, ESPN

____ Discovery Channel

____ HBO series

✓ Reality TV

9. Most likely to behave as an:

✓ Extrovert (outgoing)

____ Introvert (withdrawn)

____ Depends on the situation

2. Most likely to own a:

____ Fish

____ Cat

✓ Dog

____ Snake

____ Bird

____ Horse

4. Most likely to be:

____ Alone

____ In a crowd of friends

✓ With a few friends

____ With one other person

____ With family

6. Most likely to go to a:

✓ Live music concert

____ Play or ballet

____ Sporting event

____ Movie

____ Dance club or bar

____ Museum

8. Most likely to use:

____ Facebook

____ Twitter

✓ Snapchat

____ Instagram

____ Tumblr

____ Tinder/Grindr

____ No social media

10. Most likely to react:

____ Very emotionally

✓ Fairly emotionally/rationally

____ Very rationally

Principle 2: Using "I" Statements and Expressing Feelings

Purpose

To practice speaking descriptively instead of evaluatively and expressing feelings.

Instructions

Working as a group, rewrite each of the assigned statements using descriptive "I" language that clearly takes responsibility for the message. Then express a feeling using an emotion or feeling word. Each group should present a brief report to the rest of the class on the results of their efforts.

1. You are unreasonable.
   When you _____, I feel _____.
   Offer two possible interpretations for this behavior.

2. You are too sensitive.
   When you _____, I feel _____.
   Offer two possible interpretations for this behavior.

3. You have no respect for anyone.
   When you _____, I feel _____.
   Offer two possible interpretations for this behavior.

4. You never let me say anything.
   When you _____, I feel _____.
   Offer two possible interpretations for this behavior.

5. You never listen to a word I say.
   When you _____, I feel _____.
   Offer two possible interpretations for this behavior.

6. You're incredibly selfish.
   When you _____, I feel _____.
   Offer two possible interpretations for this behavior.

7. You're always taking and never giving.
   When you _____, I feel _____.
   Offer two possible interpretations for this behavior.

8. You're never on time for anything.
   When you _____, I feel _____.
   Offer two possible interpretations for this behavior.

9. You're sloppy.
   When you _____, I feel _____.
   Offer two possible interpretations for this behavior.

10. You never keep a promise.
    When you _____, I feel _____.
    Offer two possible interpretations for this behavior.

11. You're incredibly critical.
    When you _____, I feel _____.
    Offer two possible interpretations for this behavior.

12. You never pay any attention to me.
    When you _____, I feel _____.
    Offer two possible interpretations for this behavior.

13. You never take my side on anything.
    When you _____, I feel _____.
    Offer two possible interpretations for this behavior.

14. You never want to do the things I want to do.
    When you _____, I feel _____.
    Offer two possible interpretations for this behavior.

15. You have an attitude problem.
    When you _____, I feel _____.
    Offer two possible interpretations for this behavior.

Principle 2:   Understanding Meaning in Language

Directions

Using the concept map below, write down the first words that come to mind when thinking of the word *provided*.

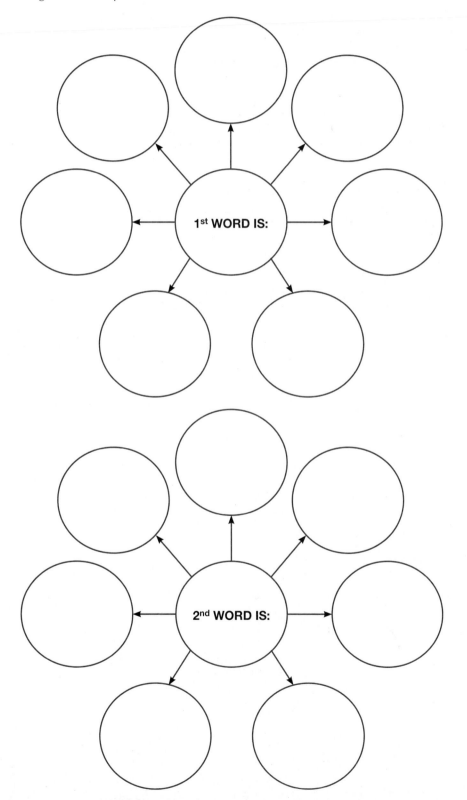

Principle 2:   Using Descriptive Language

Instructions

Below are messages that criticize in a punishing way. Come up with an alternate approach (including statements) that addresses the implied problem in a more descriptive, rather than evaluative, manner.

1. This room is a pigsty! You ought to hear what my friends say when they come in here. If you don't clean up your act, you're gonna be history!

2. What's this "C" doing on your grades? In communication? What's wrong with you?

3. What's with you this morning? Don't you get up and look in the mirror? If you can't be decent, just shut up.

4. I told you if you started dating her (him) you'd get burned, but you wouldn't listen. So don't come crying to me now. I hope you learned your lesson.

5. Look, I've had it with your being late for class. Nobody else has trouble getting here on time. If you don't care enough to be here when class starts, don't bother coming.

Principle 2:   Using Feeling Words

HAPPY

Festive	Contented	Relaxed	Calm	Complacent
Satisfied	Serene	Comfortable	Peaceful	Joyous
Ecstatic	Enthusiastic	Inspired	Glad	Pleased
Grateful	Cheerful	Excited	Cheery	Lighthearted
Buoyant	Carefree	Surprised	Optimistic	Spirited
Vivacious	Brisk	Sparkling	Merry	Generous
Hilarious	Exhilarated	Jolly	Playful	Elated
Jubilant	Thrilled	Restful	Eager	Keen
Earnest	Intent	Zealous	Ardent	Anxious
Avid	Desirous	Proud		

SAD

Sorrowful	Unhappy	Depressed	Melancholy	Gloomy
Somber	Dismal	Heavy-hearted	Quiet	Mournful
Dreadful	Dreary	Flat	Blah	Dull
In the dumps	Sullen	Moody	Sulky	Out-of-sorts
Low	Discontented	Discouraged	Disappointed	Concerned
Sympathetic	Compassionate	Choked-up	Embarrassed	Shameful
Ashamed	Useless	Worthless		

HURT

Injured	Isolated	Offended	Distressed	Pained
Suffering	Afflicted	Worried	Aching	Crushed
Heartbroken	Despairing	Torn	Lonely	Pathetic
Cold	Upset			

ANGRY

Resentful	Irritated	Enraged	Furious	Annoyed
Inflamed	Provoked	Infuriated	Offended	Sullen
Indignant	Irate	Wrathful	Cross	Sulky
Bitter	Frustrated	Grumpy	Boiling	Fuming
Stubborn	Belligerent	Confused	Awkward	Bewildered

FEARLESS

Encouraged	Courageous	Confident	Secure	Independent
Reassured	Bold	Brave	Daring	Heroic
Determined	Loyal	Proud	Impulsive	

INTERESTED

Concerned	Fascinated	Engrossed	Intrigued	Absorbed
Excited	Curious	Inquisitive	Inquiring	Creative
Sincere				

DOUBTFUL

Unbelieving	Skeptical	Distrustful	Suspicious	Dubious
Uncertain	Questioning	Evasive	Wavering	Hesitant
Perplexed	Indecisive	Hopeless	Powerless	Helpless
Defeated	Pessimistic			

PHYSICAL

Taut	Uptight	Immobilized	Paralyzed	Tense
Stretched	Hollow	Empty	Strong	Weak
Sweaty	Breathless	Nauseated	Sluggish	Weary
Repulsed	Tired	Alive	Feisty	

AFFECTIONATE

Close	Loving	Sexy	Tender	Passionate
Aggressive	Appealing	Warm		

AFRAID

Fearful	Frightened	Timid	Wishy-washy	Shaky
Apprehensive	Fidgety	Terrified	Panicky	Tragic
Hysterical	Alarmed	Cautious	Shocked	Horrified
Insecure	Impatient	Nervous	Dependent	Anxious
Pressured	Worried	Doubtful	Suspicious	Hesitant
Awed	Dismayed	Scared	Cowardly	Threatened
Appalled	Petrified	Gutless		

MISCELLANEOUS

Humble	Torn	Mixed-up	Envious	Jealous
Preoccupied	Cruel	Distant	Bored	Hypocritical
Phony	Two-faced	Cooperative		

Principle 4: Listening with a Critical Ear

Purpose

To practice listening critically.

Instructions

Here's a quick little test to determine how well you are able to separate fact from fiction. Your Lab Instructor will read a story and then you are to answer each of the 9 questions that follow the reading of the story.

How to respond to the questions: You will be presented with a series of statements. There are three possible answers for each statement. It is either a true statement or a false statement, or it does not contain enough information to draw a valid conclusion. You must respond to each statement with one of the three choices. **Circle** your choice. You will be provided the correct answers when you are finished. Each correct answer is worth 10 points.

1. A man appeared after the owner had turned off the store lights.
This Statement Is: True   Not True   Not enough information

2. The robber was a man.
This Statement Is: True   Not True   Not enough information

3. The man did not demand money.
This Statement Is: True   Not True   Not enough information

4. The store owner scooped up the contents of the cash register.
This Statement Is: True   Not True   Not enough information

5. Someone opened the cash register.
This Statement Is: True   Not True   Not enough information

6. After the man demanded money, he scooped it up and ran away.
This Statement Is: True   Not True   Not enough information

7. The story did not say how much money was in the register.
This Statement Is: True   Not True   Not enough information

8. The robber demanded money from the owner.
This Statement Is: True   Not True   Not enough information

9. Someone demanded money, a cash register was opened, its contents were scooped up, and a man ran out of the store.
This Statement Is: True   Not True   Not enough information

Adapted from William V. Haney's *Uncritical Inference Test*.

Principle 4:   Listening and Responding Thoughtfully to Others

The Listening Styles Profile Revised (LSP-R)

Instructions

Below are several items that people use to describe themselves as a listener. We would like you to assess how each statement applies to you by marking your level of agreement/disagreement with each item. The stronger you disagree with a statement, the lower the number you will enter on the line next to the statement. The stronger you agree with a statement, the higher the number you will enter. Please do not think of any specific listening situation but of your general ways of listening—how you typically listen in most situations.

1 = Strongly Disagree

2 = Disagree

3 = Somewhat Disagree

4 = Unsure

5 = Somewhat Agree

6 = Agree

7 = Strongly Agree

1. __6__ When listening to others, I am mainly concerned with how they are feeling.

2. __5__ I wait until all the facts are presented before forming judgments and opinions.

3. __3__ I am impatient with people who ramble on during conversations.

4. __6__ I often catch errors in other speakers' logic.

5. __3__ I listen to understand the emotions and mood of the speaker.

6. __5__ I fully listen to what a person has to say before forming any opinions.

7. __3__ I find it difficult to listen to people who take too long to get their idea across.

8. __5__ I naturally tend to notice errors in what other speakers say.

9. __5__ When listening to others, it is important to understand the feelings of the speaker.

10. __6__ I tend to withhold judgment about another's ideas until I have heard everything they have to say.

11. __2__ I get frustrated when people get off topic during a conversation.

12. __3__ When listening to others, I focus on any inconsistencies and/or errors in what's being said.

13. __5 6a__ I listen primarily to build and maintain relationships with others.

14. __6__ When listening to others, I attempt to withhold making an opinion until I've heard their entire message.

15. __3__ When listening to others, I become impatient when they appear to be wasting time.

16. __5__ I have a talent for catching inconsistencies in what a speaker says.

17. __6__ I enjoy listening to others because it allows me to connect with them.

18. __6__ When listening to others, I consider all sides of the issue before responding.

19. __5__ I prefer speakers who quickly get to the point.

20. __5__ When listening to others, I notice contradictions in what they say.

21. __5__ When listening to others, I focus on understanding the feelings behind the words.

22. __6__ To be fair to others, I fully listen to what they have to say before making judgments.

23. __3__ When listening to others, I appreciate speakers who give brief, to-the-point presentations.

24. __2__ Good listeners catch discrepancies in what people say.

SOURCE: Bodie, G. D., Worthington, D. L., & Gearhart, C. C. (2013). The Revised Listening Styles Profile (LSP-R): Development and validation. *Communication Quarterly, 61,* 72–90. doi:10.1080/0146333 73.2012.720343

Scoring the Listening Styles Profile Revised (LSP-R)

Scoring Instructions:

The 24-item scale measures four types of listening styles: relational listening, analytical listening, task-oriented listening, and critical listening. In the spaces below, record the number you answered for each item. Sum the column; the column with the highest number represents your preferred listening style.

Relational Listening	Analytical Listening	Task-Oriented Listening	Critical Listening
Item 1: 6	Item 2: 5	Item 3: 3	Item 4: 6
Item 5: 3	Item 6: 5	Item 7: 3	Item 8: 5
Item 9: 5	Item 10: 6	Item 11: 2	Item 12: 3
Item 13: 5	Item 14: 6	Item 15: 3	Item 16: 5
Item 17: 6	Item 18: 6	Item 19: 5	Item 20: 5
Item 21: 5	Item 22: 6	Item 23: 3	Item 24: 2
Total: 30	Total: 34	Total: 19	Total: 26

Listening Style Descriptions

- **Relational listening** = a concern with and awareness of others' feelings and emotions

- **Analytical listening** = an intentional focus on the full message of a speaker prior to forming a judgment

- **Task-oriented listening** = a concern with the amount of time spent listening as well as a desire to interact with focused speakers

- **Critical listening** = a tendency to evaluate and critically assess messages for accuracy and consistency

SOURCE: Bodie, G. D., & Worthington, D. L. (2013). Listening styles profile-revised (LSP-R). In D. L. Worthington & G. D. Bodie (Eds.), *The sourcebook of listening research: Methodology and measures.* Hoboken, NJ: John Wiley & Sons, Inc.

Principle 5:   A Cultural Prejudice Exercise

Objective

To evaluate individual and group decision-making criteria and biases.

Instructions

Imagine you are at a friend's graduation party. Because of a storm, most of the guests leave early. Suddenly you hear local sirens go off, warning you of an approaching tornado. Your friend tells you, "There's no basement, but I have a small underground cellar that will hold four people. Go get three people to go down there with you so you'll be safe. The rest of us will take our chances upstairs. Maybe we'll be lucky and the tornado will miss us." Choose the three people who will accompany you to the cellar from the following list.

List of People

- **Patrick**   is a tall, attractive, blond, 30-year-old man of Irish descent. He organized the city's Walk for Life to raise funds to help people living with AIDS. In fact, he is credited with raising over $1 million and has been honored by numerous religions and service organizations. This personable, kind, gay man has lived with HIV for several years.

- **Anna**   is 98 years old. She is of European descent and grew up in rural Arkansas as part of a huge family. Sometimes she seems narrow-minded and stubborn, but she has amazing perceptions. She has seen many things during her long life, and you appreciate her insights into the world. She has stopped you from making a mistake more than once, and you are quite fond of her.

- **Francisco**   is a Mexican government official visiting in this country. He is talented and powerful. He is friendly, outgoing, and somewhat of a wheeler-dealer, but one with a good heart and admirable motives. A good friend of your father's, this 40-year-old man seems to be able to get along with everyone. You admire his intellect, his ability to bridge the gap between the United States and Mexico, his talent to make things happen, and his friendliness. He contributes much to his country.

- **Tracy**   is 30 years old and of African decent. She has a daughter who is three and a newborn son. She lives with her parents and has recently returned to school to learn to be a beautician. Right now she's on maternity leave from school.

- **Chenu**   is a resident alien who was born in India. He is in his twenties and recently completed a doctorate in pharmaceutics. He is kind and brilliant, faces a promising career, and has a job lined up as a researcher for a pharmaceutical company in New Jersey.

- **Nina**   is in her forties. She is a Russian Jew who fled the former Soviet Union about 10 years ago with her husband and her daughter. She has struggled, but now she is on the faculty of the local college. Her daughter is attending a university in California. Her husband plays the violin with a major city symphony. She loves the United States.

- **Charlie**   just turned 13. He's a city kid who moved to the suburbs. He's of African descent and is friendly, intelligent, gentle, and courteous. He came to the party with his sister, Tracy.

- **Jack** is 21 and a college student. He comes from an upper-class family of European descent. He always seems to be in trouble. His family isn't sure whether the problem is drugs, alcohol, or mental illness. He flunks many of his courses and frequently has brushes with the law. He feels like an outcast.

COMPLETING THE EXERCISE

Write the names of the three guests you will take to the cellar here:

_____   _____   _____

Discuss the activity with the other members of your group. Here are some issues to consider:

1. What criteria did you use to decide which guests to take into the cellar?

2. How did your criteria compare to those of others in your discussion group?

3. What basic principles of problem solving could be applied to this situation?

4. What are the problems with stereotyping? To what extent do you think the preceding descriptions reinforce stereotypes?

5. Discuss the concepts of stereotyping, prejudice, political correctness, mixing of cultures, and co-cultures.

6. When doing a similar exercise in one basic communication class, one student said, "This is ridiculous. No one ever has to make these kinds of life-or-death decisions. It's a stupid exercise." Another student became very serious and impatient. "I do," the student said. "I'm a paramedic, and sometimes I come to a situation where I know I can't save everyone, and I have to decide what to do first. Just last week I went to an accident where a mother and her baby were both in critical condition. Life would be nothing for the baby if the mother died. The mother might have other children. The mother might not be able to survive knowing she was driving the car when her baby was killed. I had to decide which person I would help first." What has this activity revealed about your value system?

7. Try to reach group consensus about which three people to save.

Record your group's list of people to take to the cellar here:

_____   _____   _____

Principle 5: Diversity and Communication Assignment

The Diversity and COMM Assignment

The Diversity and Communication Assignment encourages and challenges you to examine your own positionality and identity as well as to understand the experiences of others who are different from you. You will participate in an in-class activity in which you will discuss assumptions people make about others based on various facets of their identity. The Diversity and Communication Assignment will assist you with the following competencies: **Mindfulness, Other-Orientation, Stereotyping/Prejudice, Assuming Similarity, Assuming Differences, Assuming Superiority, Listening/Asking Questions,** and **Adapting**. You will use these competencies to communicate in this growing multicultural and diverse world.

[handwritten note: ← use these terms (at least 3) Bold these in papers]

Objectives

At the end of this exercise, students will be able to

1. Submit a 1–2 page written reflection of your experience with the class activity/discussion.

2. Overcome negative expectations when communicating with strangers who are culturally dissimilar in some way.

3. Decrease the uncertainty and the anxiety that often accompanies communication interactions between culturally dissimilar individuals.

4. Realize the negative effects of prejudice and stereotyping.

5. Learn that understanding about others in an increasingly diverse world requires *effective communication*.

6. Become aware that competence in intercultural communication requires a combination of *knowledge, skills, and motivation*.

7. Be able to relate your experiences to the vocabulary in **Chapters 2** and **6** of the textbook.

Principles Targeted

1. **Be aware of your communication with yourself and others** – This assignment will challenge you to become more aware of your own identity and how you communicate with individuals who are different from you.

2. **Effectively use and interpret verbal messages** – This assignment will require you to think about the language choices you make when communicating with diverse others, such as recognizing words that may be interpreted as hurtful by diverse others.

3. **Effectively use and interpret nonverbal messages** – This assignment will require you to think about the unique nonverbal communication norms for diverse others.

4. **Listen and respond thoughtfully to others** – This assignment will challenge you to listen to different perspectives and to respond in an ethical and thoughtful manner.

5. **Appropriately adapt your messages to others** – This principle is the culmination of the assignment and will require you to specifically discuss how you will change your communication behaviors in order to appropriately adapt to those who are different from you.

Part I: Identifying Your Positionality

Instructions

First, you will need to think about your own identity and positionality. Positionality "focuses on the intersection of various aspects of a person's identity, such as race, class, and gender . . . and suggests that identity is fluid and dynamic and affected by historical and social changes" (Kezar & Lestar, 2010, p. 165).

In thinking about your positionality, please write a 1- or 2-paragraph positionality statement. Please see the next page for a few sample positionality statements. Your positionality statement should include a discussion of the following topics:

- Do your best to describe who and where you are as a person.
- How do you describe yourself demographically?
- How are you positioned in terms of race, class, gender, ethnicity/race, sexuality, nationality, religion, and ableness?
- How does your positionality impact your experiences in the world?
- How do you think your positionality impacts how you perceive the world around you?

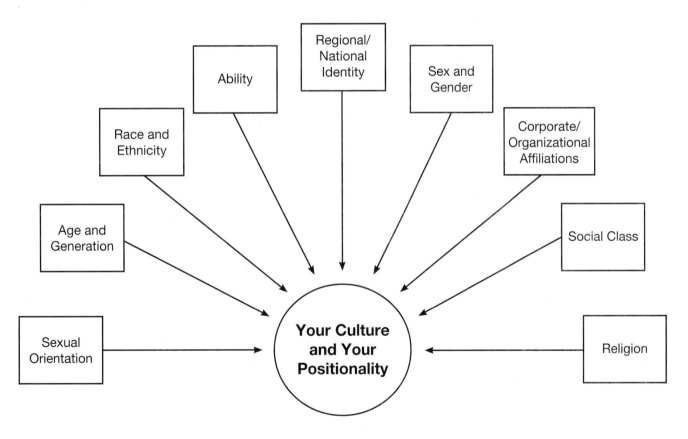

Sample Positionality Statements

As a white, upper-middle class, educated, woman, my positionality is very privileged. I grew up in a home with no mortgage and married parents. I am able-bodied and don't have to worry about money because I know my parents will have my back if I ever really get into a bind. My "womaness" is the most challenging component of my positionality. Whenever I communicate, I am much more masculine and that masculinity tends to be misconstrued as "bitchy," which reveals double standards held in our community. Beyond that, I don't consider myself a religious person, but I have never felt persecuted for my choice to not practice.

My positionality definitely impacts the way I communicate, but because of my education I have been able to study topics that encourage me to be more open-minded. Although I do sometimes feel stereotypes creeping into my mind, I do my best to challenge them and snuff them out whenever they emerge.

I am a minority in this country, and beyond that a target of many media stories right now. I am a male, Kuwaiti, Muslim, international student. My positionality is unique and contributes to not only the way I interact with others, but especially the way others interact with me. Right now there are many misconceptions about Muslims and Middle-Easterners, and I often feel these uncertainties coming from other people whenever they are communicating with me. After talking to me and getting to know me one afternoon, someone once told me, "I could never consider you a terrorist." Obviously.

I am very privileged because I am in the United States studying. This is due to the wealth of my country. I recognize that merely a hundred years ago my grandpa lived in a mud house, and what I have now is so much.

My Positionality Statement

Instructions

Use the space below to write your own positionality statement.

_____

_____

_____

_____

Part II: In-class Activity

Instructions

Please recall an incident when an individual made a hurtful or upsetting assumption about your identity. Select a partner with whom you feel comfortable sharing this incident. Be sure to discuss why the incident was upsetting to you.

_____

_____

_____

_____

_____

_____

Create a placard in the space under the line below that embraces or rejects these assumptions. You will share this aloud with the class.

· ·

Part III: Reflection Paper

Instructions

After participating in the in-class activity, you will write a 1–2 page reflection paper.

- Include an introductory paragraph that captures the reader's attention and includes a complete thesis statement.
- Include all of the following in the body of your paper:
  1. What you took away from the in-class activity.
  2. A clear description of your positionality.
  3. A discussion of similarities and differences between your experiences and the experiences of your classmates.
  4. A discussion of the consequences of NOT adapting communication to others.
  5. A thoughtful discussion of the impact this assignment will have on your future choices and actions regarding intercultural communication.
  6. A discussion of specific strategies for developing knowledge, motivation, and skill to adapt to others.
- As you respond to these items, include **at least 3 multicultural terms** included in **Chapter 6** of your textbook (**Mindfulness, Other-Orientation, Stereotyping/ Prejudice, Assuming Similarity, Assuming Differences, Assuming Superiority, Listening/Asking Questions,** and **Adapting**). **Bold** these terms in your paper.
- As you respond to these items, please make sure that your paper is written in a culturally sensitive manner. If your paper is deemed inappropriate, you will earn either significant grade deductions or a zero on this assignment.
- End with a concluding paragraph that pulls everything together and reflects the introduction.
- Submit an electronic version of your paper in Word format to Turnitin.com via the Assignments tab on your course's TRACS site.
- Ask your instructor if they would like a hard copy of your paper as well.
- If so, staple the assessment instrument to the front of your paper.

Part IV: Optional Diversity Role Extra Credit Opportunity

- Find 3–4 students who would like to participate in this extra credit activity:
  - ❑ Student One:
  - ❑ Student Two:
  - ❑ Student Three:
  - ❑ Student Four:
- Schedule a 1-hour visit with the COMM lab.
- The sign-up process is in the Guidebook.
- Two students will have to sign up for consecutive ½-hour appointments, so that you have a full 1-hour appointment.

  - Student One: _____   Time Scheduled: _____

  - Student Two: _____   Time Scheduled: _____

*Go to the COMM Lab (Alkek Library Room 480A) and bring your completed placard. You will each discuss the meaning of your placard and then engage in a brief discussion. The discussion is similar to, but more in depth than the one you do in class.

*The lab facilitator will give your information to your instructor, and you will be awarded extra credit points (5 points).

*This extra credit opportunity MUST be completed before the second exam.

Preparing for Exams in Comm 1310

General Information

The following general information will be useful in preparing for exams in this class:

- Examinations will be administered in class on the days announced by your instructor.

- Examinations will consist of multiple-choice, objective-based items.

- For examinations you will need to bring with you a #2 pencil. Your instructor will provide you with an answer sheet.

- Examinations will each consist of 50 items worth two points each.

- Examination items will be of two types: "lower order" items that require simple recall of a term, definition, principle, or concept; and "higher order" items that require differentiation or application of a term, definition, or principle.

General Preparation

Your score on each exam will almost certainly be higher if you follow these suggestions:

- Read each chapter in the textbook when it is assigned and answer the questions listed on the study guides for each chapter (see **next section**). Waiting until the night before the examination to read the chapters for the first time will likely produce information overload.

- Take careful notes during class. Examples and illustrations provided in lecture and in lab will help you in understanding and applying terms, definitions, principles, and concepts.

- Before the examination, review each chapter from the textbook as well as your class notes. Examination items may be based either on the chapters or on lecture content.

- It is not enough simply to know the textbook definitions of terms. You must also be able to distinguish between similar concepts.

- Complete the sample test items on the following pages.

Study Guide for Principles of Communication Module

Chapter 1 Foundations of Human Communication

1. Be able to **recall** and **explain** the three criteria that are used to assess someone's communication competence.
2. Be able to **identify** and **define** the components of the communication process, including source, encoding, decoding, receiver, message, channel, noise, feedback, and context.
3. Be able to **differentiate** between the three models of communication: communication as action, communication as interaction, and communication as transaction.
4. Be able to **identify** and **define** the five characteristics of communication.
5. Be able to **differentiate** between the five fundamental Communication Principles for a Lifetime outlined by Beebe, Beebe, and Ivy.

Chapter 2 Self Awareness and Communication

1. Be able to **differentiate** between self-concept and self-esteem.
2. Be able to **define** and **identify** examples of James' three selves (material, social, spiritual)
3. Be able to **describe** the four factors that affect the development of self-concept.
4. Be able to **identify** and **explain** the three stages of the perception process.
5. Be able to **identify** three ways to improve our ability to form accurate perceptions.
6. Be able to **describe** and **identify** examples of indirect and direct perception checking.
7. Be able to **identify** the four factors affecting self-esteem.
8. Be able to **differentiate** between avowed and ascribed identity.

Chapter 3 Understanding Verbal Messages

1. Be able to **identify** examples of bypassing language.
2. Be able to **differentiate** between connotative and denotative meanings and identify examples of both.
3. Be able to **differentiate** between concrete and abstract language.
4. Be able to **identify** five ways words have power, including the Sapir-Whorf hypothesis.
5. Be able to **differentiate** between descriptive and evaluative verbal messages.
6. Be able to **differentiate** between empathic and detached verbal messages.
7. Be able to **differentiate** between superior and equal verbal messages.
8. Be able to **identify** gunnysacking as a defensive communication.

Chapter 4 Understanding Nonverbal Messages

1. Be able to **identify** examples of the six functions of nonverbal communication: substituting, complementing, conflicting, repeating, regulating, and accenting.
2. Be able to **explain** the nature of nonverbal communication and how it is culture-bound, rule-governed, ambiguous, continuous, non-linguistic, and multichanneled.
3. Be able to **identify** examples of and differentiate between nonverbal codes, including appearance/artifacts, body movements, posture, eye contact, facial expressions, haptics, vocalics, physical environment, space, and territory.

Chapter 5 Listening and Responding

1. Be able to **differentiate** between hearing and listening.
2. Be able to **identify** examples of the five activities of listening, including selecting, attending, understanding, remembering, and responding.
3. Be able to **identify** the four listening styles.
4. Be able to **identify** examples of the three major listening barriers, including self-barriers, information-processing barriers, and context barriers.
5. Be able to **differentiate** between the three-step process (stop–look–listen) for improving your listening skills.
6. Be able to **identify** the strategies for improving responding skills, including paraphrasing content and emotions.

Chapter 6 Adapting to Others: Diversity and Communication

1. Be able to **differentiate** between the four forms of human diversity.
2. Be able to **differentiate** between high-context and low-context cultures.
3. Be able to **differentiate** between the various cultural values of: decentralized and centralized, individualistic and collectivistic, and indulgent and restrained expectations about happiness.
4. Be able to **differentiate** between masculine (instrumental), feminine (expressive), and androgynous orientations.
5. Be able to **list** and **identify** the five barriers to bridging communicative differences and adapting to others, including assuming superiority, assuming similarity, assuming differences, and stereotyping and prejudice.
6. Be able to **define** intercultural communication competence and the strategies for developing knowledge, motivation, and skill.

Sample Exam Questions
Module: Principles of Communication

Chapter 1   Foundations of Human Communication

1. Acting on information is defined as _____. Making sense out of the world and sharing that sense with others through verbal and nonverbal messages is defined as _____.

    A. Human communication; communication
    B. Communication; human communication
    C. Responding; human communication
    D. Communication; responding

2. The pathway through which messages pass between source and receiver is called:

    A. Channel
    B. Context
    C. Noise
    D. Feedback

3. Henry was involved in a heated argument with his girlfriend Samantha and made some very hurtful comments to her. The next day he called Samantha to tell her that he didn't really mean what he'd said. Samantha, however, couldn't forgive Henry because she kept recalling his hurtful words. According to the "Characteristics of Communication," Samantha is demonstrating that communication is:

    A. Inescapable
    B. Complicated
    C. Irreversible
    D. Rule-governed

4. Tom and Steve are discussing the quiz they just took in class. As Tom shares his ideas, Steve holds his response until Tom has finished speaking. Steve then answers Tom's questions and adds his own information. This situation best describes which model of human communication?

    A. Action
    B. Interaction
    C. Reaction
    D. Transaction

5. Jason meets with three of his friends everyday to discuss reading assignments from a class. He is engaging in what type of communication with his friends?

    A. Interpersonal
    B. Public
    C. Impersonal
    D. Small group

Chapter 2   Self Awareness and Communication

1. Judy is a pool player. She has been involved in the sport for 6 years and has never won any tournaments. Her parents tell her she is one of the best pool players they have ever seen, and Judy feels very confident about her talent. Judy's self-concept has developed through:

    A. Self-image
    B. Communication with others
    C. Self-labels
    D. Assumed roles

2. Before his exam, Chad felt nervous and unprepared. He told his friend, "I think that I am going to fail." When Chad got his exam score back, he earned a failing grade. This scenario is an example of:

    A. Self-concept
    B. Self-fulfilling prophecy
    C. Self-image
    D. Self-expectations

3. Luke is driving his car to the grocery store. The music is playing, his wife is talking to him on his cell phone, and the a/c is buzzing. Luke begins to sing the words to the song on the radio. Which stage of perception has Luke engaged in?

    A. Attention
    B. Interpretation
    C. Selection
    D. Organization

4. To improve your ability to form accurate perceptions of others, you should:

    A. Make generalizations about others
    B. Check your perceptions of others
    C. Allow stereotypes to influence your actions
    D. Trust your first impressions of others

5. Kim tells her roommate, "Our apartment is really messy with your clothes on the floor and dirty dishes stacked up in the sink. I don't know if you are so busy with school that you haven't had time to clean up, or if you are hoping that I will clean up after you. What is the reason?" Kim's statement is an example of:

    A. Indirect perception checking
    B. Intrapersonal communication
    C. Direct perception checking
    D. Stereotyping

Chapter 3   Understanding Verbal Messages

1. Sarah and John agreed to meet early before class to review their notes. Sarah arrived 30 minutes before class. When John arrived five minutes before class, Sarah said, "I thought you were going to come to class early." John replied, "I am early." The word "early" in this scenario is an example of what type of language?

    A. Bypassing
    B. Restrictive
    C. Denotative
    D. Concrete

2. The Sapir-Whorf Hypothesis is a theory that helps us better explain the impor-
    tance of which of the fundamental communication principles below?

    A. Be aware of your communication with yourself and others
    B. Effectively use and interpret verbal messages
    C. Listen and respond thoughtfully to others
    D. Appropriately adapt messages to others

3. A word's literal meaning is _____. A word's subjective meaning is _____.

    A. Connotative; denotative
    B. Denotative; abstract
    C. Concrete; abstract
    D. Denotative; connotative

4. When Jack said to his girlfriend Nancy, "You know, I'm tired of you never pay-
    ing attention to me and ignoring what I want. You either care about me or you
    don't." Jack's comments to Nancy exhibit that words have the power to:

    A. Affect thought and actions
    B. Make or break relationships
    C. Create and label experiences
    D. Shape and reflect culture

5. Juan and Courtney are in a healthy argument over which political candidate is
    better. He tells Courtney, "I may be wrong, but here's something you might want
    to consider before you vote . . . " Juan is establishing a supportive relationship by
    doing which of the following:

    A. Describing his own feelings rather than evaluating others
    B. Empathizing rather than remaining detached from others
    C. Presenting himself as equal rather than superior
    D. Being flexible rather than rigid toward others

Chapter 4   Understanding Nonverbal Messages

1. When the professor stated, "We must begin class," she also pounded her fist on
    the desk when she said "must." Her gesture serves which nonverbal function?

    A. Substituting
    B. Complementing
    C. Accenting
    D. Repeating

2. Chris knew that Matt was lying to him when he said that he did not have time
    to help him move into his new apartment in Chicago. He saw Matt look down,
    heard his voice get softer, and watched him shift uncomfortably in his chair.
    Which element of nonverbal communication was Chris observing?

    A. Nonverbal communication is rule governed
    B. Nonverbal communication is continuous
    C. Nonverbal communication is multichanneled
    D. Nonverbal communication is ambiguous

3. The study of human movements, posture, and gestures can be defined as:

    A. Nonverbal cues
    B. Illustrators
    C. Kinesics
    D. Haptics

4. There is a group of girls in elementary school sitting at a table during lunchtime. The girls put their lunch boxes up on their sides to make a barrier between themselves and the boys who sit across from them. The girls' lunch boxes demonstrate the use of:

   A. Environmental markers
   B. Territorial markers
   C. Personal space
   D. Social space

5. Marcus has a tattoo on his arm that says "Men Rule." When Joan saw this, she moved to the other side of the classroom because it offended her. Marcus' tattoo served as a/an _____ nonverbal code.

   A. Attractiveness
   B. Dress
   C. Illustrator
   D. Artifact

Chapter 5   Listening and Responding

1. Assigning meaning to messages occurs in which step of the listening process?

   A. Selecting
   B. Attending
   C. Understanding
   D. Remembering

2. Brian is thinking about what he is going to say to his girlfriend while he is looking at her and listening to her. Which of the following barriers to listening is Brian experiencing?

   A. Self-focus
   B. Emotional noise
   C. Criticism
   D. Processing rate

3. Doug and Renee are talking in the quad. Renee is describing the exam that she has just completed in her Marketing class while Doug listens. To gain a complete understanding of what she is saying, Doug shifts the focus away from his own thoughts and attempts to experience the thoughts of Renee. Doug is engaged in:

   A. Empathizing
   B. Decentering
   C. Sympathizing
   D. Adapting

4. Restating in your own words what you think the other person is saying is called:

   A. Understanding your partner's feelings
   B. Paraphrasing the content
   C. Paraphrasing the emotions
   D. Asking appropriate questions

5. Emma tells her friend Chelsee about an argument that she had with her boyfriend. Chelsee is listening for facts and realizes Emma is contradicting herself. Which listening style is Chelsee using here?

   A. Analytical
   B. Relational
   C. Critical
   D. Task-oriented

Chapter 6   Adapting to Others: Diversity and Communication

1. When individuals or groups of individuals from different cultures communicate, they are engaging in what type of communication?

    A. Co-cultural
    B. Intercultural
    C. Cultural
    D. Bi-cultural

2. North Americans tend to rely more on verbal messages and use less contextual cues. North Americans are an example of:

    A. Cultural context
    B. Cultural values
    C. High-context culture
    D. Low-context culture

3. In these cultures, every member of a team is rewarded for good work and punished for poor work, takes responsibility for completing an assignment, and sees decisions as they would affect the entire team. This type of culture is referred to as:

    A. Individualistic
    B. Masculine
    C. Feminine
    D. Collectivistic

4. Jennifer was raised in the South and is extremely outgoing and friendly. Although 90% of the people who work in Jennifer's new office are from different parts of the country than she and interact in very unusual ways (e.g., keep to themselves; rarely make eye contact), she continues to engage in her Southern ways. She visits their desks throughout the work day and attempts to engage them in friendly one-on-one conversations. What stage of intercultural competence would best describe Jennifer's behavior with her co-workers?

    A. Stage One: Denial
    B. Stage Four: Acceptance
    C. Stage Three: Minimize
    D. Stage Six: Integration

5. Hillary brought her Japanese friend, Nayoko, home to visit her grandparents. When Nayoko addressed Hillary's grandmother as "Mrs. Winn," Hillary's grandmother said, "Oh, please call me Mary." Nayoko became very uncomfortable and thereafter avoided addressing Mrs. Winn at all. Never in Nayoko's experiences had she ever addressed a friend's grandparent by her first name; it would be considered an insult in her culture. Which barrier did Mrs. Winn most likely encounter in this situation?

    A. Assuming superiority
    B. Assuming similarity
    C. Assuming differences
    D. Stereotyping and prejudice

Answer Key

CHAPTER 1

1. B
2. A
3. C
4. B
5. D

CHAPTER 2

1. B
2. B
3. C
4. B
5. C

CHAPTER 3

1. A
2. B
3. D
4. B
5. D

CHAPTER 4

1. C
2. C
3. C
4. B
5. D

CHAPTER 5

1. C
2. A
3. B
4. B
5. C

CHAPTER 6

1. B
2. D
3. D
4. C
5. B

MODULE 2
COMMUNICATING IN THE INTERPERSONAL CONTEXT

After completing this module (Chapters 7 and 8 and the Guidebook PUGSS Supplement), you will be able to:

PRINCIPLE 1
Be aware of your communication with yourself and others.

- Explain how self-perceptions (self-concept and self-esteem) influence interpersonal communication and are affected by it.
- Recognize relational aspects of power.
- Identify and explain eleven stages of relational escalation and de-escalation.
- Identify your own conflict style (nonconfrontational, confrontational, cooperative), and understand how your style influences communication about conflict.
- Identify and describe four components of interpersonal conflict: expressed struggle, perceived incompatible goals, perceived scarce rewards/resources, and interdependence.
- Recognize the pervasiveness of culture and its influence on interpersonal communication.
- Explain and/or apply uncertainty reduction and social penetration theories.

PRINCIPLE 2
Effectively use and interpret verbal messages.

- Identify and demonstrate understanding of interpersonal conflict by applying the PUGSS model: Describe Problem, Achieve Understanding, Identify Goals, Brainstorm Solutions, Select Best Solution.
- Differentiate constructive verbal conflict management strategies from destructive verbal conflict management strategies: description versus evaluation, and assertiveness/argumentativeness versus aggressiveness.

- Self-disclose emotions and feelings.
- Differentiate qualities of self-disclosure: amount, positive–negative, depth, and honesty–accuracy.
- Apply guidelines for appropriate self-disclosure.

PRINCIPLE 3
Effectively use and interpret nonverbal messages.

- Demonstrate and recognize appropriate nonverbal responsive behaviors.
- Differentiate constructive nonverbal conflict management strategies from destructive conflict management strategies: responsiveness versus nonresponsiveness or avoidance.
- Perception check others' nonverbal behavior to insure accurate interpretation.

PRINCIPLE 4
Listen and respond thoughtfully to others.

- Differentiate paraphrasing of content from paraphrasing of emotions.
- Create appropriate paraphrases to check understanding of content and emotions.

PRINCIPLE 5
Appropriately adapt messages to others.

- Differentiate interpersonal communication in high-context cultures from low-context cultures.
- Recognize how gender influences interpersonal communication.
- Identify and overcome barriers that prevent appropriate adaptation.

Chapter 7
Lecture Notes

Chapter 8
Lecture Notes

Understanding Self-disclosure Properties

Instructions:

Please answer the following questions after reading through the scenarios below:

1. How are the three properties of self-disclosure (reciprocity, appropriateness, risk) exemplified in the scenario? Explain.

2. Is the disclosure more or less likely to enhance the interpersonal relationship described in the scenario? Why or why not?

3. How would *you* manage the self-disclosure in the scenario? Explain the best course of action for communicating this information.

Scenario 1

Gabby recounted a detailed story about her recent operation in an email to her co-worker, Aliyah. Although she has only been working at XYZ company for 2 months, she and Aliyah have gone to lunch together once and they regularly discuss projects at work. When she didn't get a response to her initial email, Gabby emailed Aliyah a second time, attaching a photo of herself in the hospital recovery room. This time, Aliyah responded, "I hope you are feeling better. Did you see the email about the new project for our marketing team?"

Scenario 2

Hunter and his bandmate, Caleb, have been touring together for the past three summers. Last year, they decided to get an apartment together. After their final performance this summer, Caleb confided in Hunter that his older sister had become addicted to drugs and that he and his parents were staging an intervention the next day. He asked Hunter if he had ever been confronted with a similar situation and if he had any advice.

Scenario 3

Jackson and Candice decided to go on a date after having met at a campus party. Jackson is active in Texas State's College Democrats club and is passionate about state and local politics. During their dinner together, Jackson tells Candice that he cannot understand how anyone voted for their state Senator in the most recent election. He uses expletives to describe the senator and characterizes anyone who supported her as uninformed, stupid, and just plain "crazy."

Scenario 4

Kassandra and her girlfriend, Meredith, just got into an argument because Kassandra is jealous of how much time Meredith spends with her ex (even though Meredith swears they are just friends). Kassandra told a mutual friend of theirs what happened, and Meredith was angry when she found out that Kassandra shared the information about their conflict with someone outside of their relationship.

Scenario 5

Cory has dyslexia, a learning disability that affects his ability to read and interpret written words. After performing poorly on his first exam, his instructor, Dr. Malcolm, asked Cory to visit during his office hours to discuss strategies for improvement. Cory is unsure whether he should disclose his learning disability because he is not registered with the Office of Disability Services and does not like to tell others about this difficulty.

Self-disclosure Exercise

Purpose:

1. To understand the importance of self-disclosure in relational development.

2. To understand both the difficulty and appropriateness (or inappropriateness) of disclosing intimate information.

Instructions:

During the time allotted for this experience, you are to ask questions from this list. The questions vary in terms of their intimacy, and you may want to begin with some relatively less intimate ones. You may take turns initiating the questions. You must follow these rules: 1) Your communication with your partner will be held in confidence. 2) Any question that you ask your partner you must be willing to answer yourself. 3) You may decline to answer any question initiated by your partner. When you are finished asking questions from the list, answer the five questions at the end.

Questions:

- How important is religion in your life?
- What is the source of your financial income?
- What are your favorite hobbies or leisure interests?
- What do you feel most ashamed of in your past?
- What is your grade-point average at present?
- Have you deliberately lied about a serious matter to either parent?
- How do you feel about couples living together without being married?
- Have you been arrested or fined for violating any law?
- What do you regard as your chief fault in personality?
- How do you feel about interracial dating or marriage?
- Do you consider yourself a liberal or conservative with regard to political parties?
- What turns you off the fastest?
- What features of your appearance do you consider most attractive to members of the opposite sex?
- What do you regard as your least attractive features?
- How important is money to you?
- Are you or your parents divorced? Have you ever considered divorce?
- To what clubs do you belong?
- What person would you most like to take a trip with right now?
- Do you drink alcoholic beverages?
- How do you feel about swearing?
- Have you ever been drunk?
- Do you enjoy manipulating or directing people?
- Are females equal, inferior, or superior to males?
- How often have you needed to see a doctor in the past year?
- Would you participate in a public demonstration?
- What emotions do you find most difficult to control?

- Is there a particular person you wish would be attracted to you?
- What foods do you most dislike?
- What is your IQ?
- Is there any feature of your personality that you are proud of? What is it?
- What was your worst failure in life, your biggest disappointment to yourself or to your family?
- What is your favorite TV program(s)?
- What is your most chronic problem at present?
- What is the subject of the most serious quarrels you have had with your parents?
- What is the subject of your most frequent daydream?
- How are you feeling about me?
- What are your career goals?
- With what do you feel the greatest need for help?
- What were you most punished or criticized for when you were a child?
- How do you feel about crying in the presence of others?
- What activities did you take part in during high school?
- How could you improve your present living arrangement?
- Do you have any misgivings about the group so far?
- What is your main complaint about the group?
- Do you like your name?
- If you could be anything/anyone—besides yourself—what/who would you be?

Instructions:

After working with your partner, answer the following questions.

1. What were the easiest questions to ask?

hobbies/interests', clubs, what they did in high school

2. What were the easiest questions to answer?

fav TV Program, Career goals

3. What was harder—sharing in same-sex or different-sex dyads?

different - sex

4. How do you feel about this person now compared to others in the class?

she's great, I know her more

5. Do you (did you) self-disclose to this person?

yes

6. How many of you asked the riskiest question first? Why or why not?

No, because I wanted to start easy & then get to the riskier stuff

Relational Escalation

Pg 175
- Pink box
Pg 177
- Pink box

Intimacy – recognized in public together / get self concepts from the other person

Intensification – inside jokes / talk more like the person.

Exploration – more indepth convo

Initiation – asking questions? talk to them

Pre-Interaction Awareness – become aware of your attraction
knowing that you exsist
– social media

Relational De-Escalation

Turmoil — Conflict/take partners for granted

Stagnation

De-Intensification — When partners decrease interaction

Individualization — define lives as individuals

Separation

Post Interaction — affects how you look at future relationships

PUGSS
Structuring Conflict Management Skills

PUGSS Guidebook Supplement

By Steven A. Beebe and Timothy P. Mottet

Conflict happens. Even in the best of relationships you will inevitably discover that you will disagree with your friend, colleague, family member, or lover about something. The goal of our discussion of conflict is not how to avoid it or eliminate it from our relationships, but how to manage it so that our disagreements with others don't result in angry shouting matches and severed relationships. As stated in your text, interpersonal conflict occurs when two people cannot agree on a way to meet their needs. You know you're involved in conflict with someone when there is an *expressed struggle* (verbal or nonverbal) between individuals who are **interdependent**. The verbal expression of disagreement may range from a mild, "I'm sorry, but I believe you've made a mistake," to a stinging string of shouted obscenities that attack a person's dignity and self worth. Nonverbally, the conflict may be signaled with a momentary flash of a frown or engaged fists. Conflict is most likely to occur when one person's gain results in an unfair loss for another person. *Perceived scarce rewards/resources, perceived incompatible goals*, and a *climate of competition* rather than cooperation are also conflict triggers. Conflict can sometimes be a challenge to manage because of the interdependent nature of interpersonal relationships. By interdependence, we mean the satisfaction of one person in the relationship depends upon the actions of the other person. What you do or say affects both you and your partner; your partner's comments and actions affect you. One person cannot just independently decide the conflict is over; managing conflict is a collaborative, interdependent process.

What's your approach to dealing with interpersonal conflict? Do you generally use an in-your-face confrontational approach to sorting out differences with others? Such an approach assumes someone must win and someone must lose. Another approach is to be nonconfrontational. Some people don't like to make a scene and would rather withdraw or avoid conflict. Or, because they dislike any type of conflict, they quickly change the subject or make an extra effort to please the other person rather than deal directly with what's causing the conflict.

Your textbook, *Communication: Principles for a Lifetime*, suggests a third approach— a cooperative approach. Rather than viewing conflict as something to be ignored or an opportunity to gain the upper hand, the cooperative approach views conflict as a set of problems to be solved. Conflict is not a competition that must be won; it involves issues that should be discussed with an eye toward finding a mutually acceptable solution. The underlying principles for the cooperative style of conflict include:

1. *Separate the people from the problem:* Don't make the conflict personal; keep the discussion focused on issues rather than personalities.

2. *Focus on shared interests:* Seek to identify goals and objectives common to all people involved in the conflict.

3. *Generate many options to solve the problem:* Rather than arguing over just one possible solution, try to find many different ways to achieve the goal.

4. *Base decisions on objective criteria:* Identify what you're looking for in a solution. Clearly spell out what everyone needs in order to be satisfied with a solution.

Your textbook also suggests specific communication skills to develop a cooperative communication style with others: manage emotions, manage information, manage goals, and manage the problem. To help you structure how to use these conflict management skills when a cooperative style is the appropriate way to manage conflict, we present a specific sequence or structure to help you use these communication strategies. A cooperative style of conflict can be achieved if you do the following:

1. Clearly describe the problem that is causing the conflict in a calm, rational way.

2. Achieve understanding to ensure that you and your partner are clearly talking about the same things in terms that make sense to both of you.

3. Identify your goals. Determine what you're looking for as well as what your partner is looking for in terms of a solution to the problem.

4. Brainstorm solutions. Generate several possible ways to achieve your goals rather than arguing about just one option.

5. Select the best solution. After considering the alternatives, select a solution that best achieves your goals.

This sequence of skills can thus be succinctly summarized in five steps: problem, understanding, goals, solutions, and best solution. To help you remember these steps, use the acronym **PUGSS** (**P**roblem, **U**nderstanding, **G**oal, **S**olutions, and **S**olution). Let's take a closer look at these five steps and integrate the communication principles and skills discussed in the text to help you structure a conflict management discussion where cooperation rather than confrontation or nonconfrontation is the preferred style.

Describe the Problem

It clearly states in the syllabus that your instructor will accept your paper until 5:00 PM. You drop your paper off at the department office at 4:45 PM pleased with yourself that you have 15 minutes to spare in meeting the deadline. Yet when you receive your paper back from your instructor, you've been docked one letter grade for a late paper. You are not pleased. In fact, you're angry. What's the best way to approach your instructor? Our suggestion: Use the first step in the PUGSS process. Calmly describe the *problem* to your instructor. Although you're angry, upset, and confused, we don't recommend that you ambush your teacher at the end of class and blurt out, "You're wrong! You docked my paper when I had it in on time." A kinder, gentler, more rational approach usually gets the best results. Frame the situation as a problem to be solved rather than a battle to be won.

Your emotional reaction is often one of the first signs that you are having a conflict with someone. Anger and frustration are the typical emotions that you experience when you feel you've not been treated fairly or your entitled to something that you didn't receive—two very powerful conflict triggers. Responding with emotional volatility, however, usually does not produce positive results; instead of helping to manage the conflict it often increases feelings of anger and resentment for both you and the other person. What seems to work best is to clearly describe the problem that's fueling your emotional intensity. We acknowledge that there may be times when it's appropriate to express your anger and frustration. In those situations make your expression of emotions a conscious decision rather than the default position. Mindlessly "speaking your mind" may make you momentarily feel better, however, it may not help manage the problem.

In chapter 3 of your text, "Understanding Verbal Messages," you learned that it's better to describe your feelings to others than to evaluate them. One of the strategies that can help you describe the problem rather than begin by evaluating or attacking your partner is to use what is called an "I" message rather than a "you" message. Statements that begin with the word "you" often have an edge or bite to them. "You never liked me." "You're always late." "You always leave the kitchen in such a mess." These "you" messages are likely to create an emotional backlash and instead of helping to describe the problem at hand, may result in an escalation of anger and frustration.

A better approach is to use an "I" message: Make the first word of your sentence "I" rather than "you." This takes an edge off the statement by making your message more a description of how you feel rather than an accusatory, attacking message. Here are some "I" message examples: "I feel like you don't care about me when you are late." "I find it hard to cook my own meal when I find the kitchen in such a mess." With your instructor whom you believe gave you an undeserved lower grade on your paper you could say, "I'm confused. I don't understand why my grade was lowered when I turned in the paper 15 minutes before the deadline." An "I" message is usually a better way to describe a problem rather than an accusatory "you" message; with an "I" message you are owning the problem rather than implying that the other person is automatically guilty or is purposely trying to deny you your rights before he or she has a chance to talk with you.

In addition to using "I" messages remember the other strategies for managing emotions mentioned in your text: Select a mutually acceptable time and place to discuss a conflict. Plan your message. Monitor your nonverbal messages. Avoid personal attacks, name-calling, profanity, and emotional overstatement. Use self-talk to help you remain focused on describing the problem at hand.

Achieve Understanding ✳*most* important **Step**

After you've described the problem that's creating the conflict, don't immediately start searching for solutions and demanding change. The "U" in PUGSS stands for *understanding*. Seek to be understood and listen to the other person. One way to facilitate understanding is to ask the other person, "Do you understand why I believe there is a problem?" If you've done a good job of using "I" messages to describe the problem, you'll have gone a long way toward facilitating understanding. If the other person becomes defensive and becomes angry and upset, it is especially important to be descriptive rather than evaluative.

Listening skills are crucial to ensuring that understanding occurs. One way to foster good listening skills is to be a good listener yourself. After you have described the problem and stated how you are feeling, let the other person talk. Don't interrupt him or her. Just listen.

Another effective strategy that promotes understanding is to selectively and appropriately paraphrase what the other person is saying to make sure you understand his or her point. As noted in your text, you don't need to parrot every word or statement; instead, selectively summarize key points to make sure you understand what the other person is saying. If you or your partner is emotionally upset, paraphrasing will be hard to do. That's why it will be important to manage your emotions. We don't tend to listen very well when we're emotionally upset. But paraphrasing can be a useful way of slowing down a rapidly escalating conflict situation. To achieve understanding take your time.

How do you know if you need to paraphrase to clarify a misunderstanding? Often the other person's nonverbal cues will tip you off that additional clarification may be needed. A frown, decreased eye contact, a smirking look of disgust, or anxious fidgeting may suggest that your partner is upset or is not in agreement with your message. Seeking clarity about the nonverbal expressions of disagreement may help you enhance the accuracy of your message.

Your textbook discussed the skill of perception checking in Chapter 2. Direct perception checking is the skill of asking someone whether your interpretation of his or her behavior is correct. If, for example, during a discussion you seem to be making progress but you see your colleague fold her arms and frown as well as hear a touch of sarcasm in her voice. To check your perceptions you could say, "I get the feeling from your frown that you're not very happy with my proposal," or, "You said you agree, but the tone of your voice sounds like you disagree. Are you still upset with me?" Being aware of nonverbal expressions and then using those nonverbal cues to check your perceptions can help enhance your understanding and your partner's meaning of a message. But just as we suggested you shouldn't overuse the paraphrasing skill, so too don't go overboard on using the perception checking skill. Check your perceptions when you really aren't sure what your partner means. Overusing the skill may only make matters worse if your partner feels you're trying to manipulate him or her.

Using these communication skills should allow your relational partner to answer "yes" to your question: "Do you understand why I believe there is a problem?" If your partner says, "No, I don't know what the big deal is," or "No, I don't think there is a problem," then it's important to <u>return</u> to the "P" in PUGSS and continue describing the problem. You will not be successful in managing the conflict if your relational partner doesn't understand the problem. Here's an opportunity to adapt your message. Principle Five reminds us that we should continuously adapt our message to others. Describe the problem from a different angle or from a different perspective. Adapt your descriptive language. What does the problem look, smell, feel, sound, and taste like?

Appropriately adapting your communication should allow your relational partner to understand the problem. Once you achieve understanding, you're ready for the "G" in PUGSS or identify goals.

Identify **G**oals

After you've describe the problem and you and your partner understand the issues involved, the next step (the "G" in PUGSS) is to clarify the *goals*. Identify what you want as well as your partner's goals. Remember, it's essential that you don't try to clarify your goals until you understand one another. If you aren't sure your partner understands the issues involved in the conflict, you'll need to approach the problem from a different perspective.

Once you believe you understand the conflict issues, how do you identify goals during conflict? As suggested in your text, there are two steps. First, clarify what your goals are as well as determine your partner's goal. Then, identify where your goals and your partner's goals overlap.

To identify your goal, reflect on what the underlying problem is that is fueling the conflict. Is the conflict the result of perceived scarce rewards/resources? Do you or your partner feel that someone is taking something from you to which you are entitled? In many roommate conflict situations, the perceived scarce rewards/resources include space (proxemics), money, and quiet time. If you had more room, more money, and less noise, you wouldn't have a problem. Be able to identify and describe your personal goals. What resources/rewards do you need that would help alleviate the conflict situation?

In the example of your instructor who lowered your grade by assuming you didn't meet the deadline, your goal is to be successful in college so that you can obtain the job/career you desire. The trickier part is to consider your partner's goals. To accomplish this task, you'll need to be empathic; you'll need to consider the issues and emotions involved from your partner's point of view. If, for example, you determine that the goal of your instructor is to be a good teacher who evaluates students fairly, then you are beginning to develop a framework for searching for a solution to the problem.

After you've clarified your goals and your partner's goals, you can begin searching for how your goals and your partner's overlap and identify what underlying values your goals and your partner's goals have in common. In the case of you and your instructor, both goals involve fairness and accomplishing the academic work in the course. The challenge in managing conflict is to find a way to achieve your mutual goals rather than merely arguing over differences of opinion. Focusing on shared interests (common goals) is an essential strategy for managing the conflict.

Brainstorm **S**olutions

When both parties understand the problem and have an idea of the underlying goals of each person involved in the conflict, you can now turn your attention to finding possible solutions to the problem. The first "S" in PUGSS is to brainstorm *solutions*. Rather than arm wrestling over just one solution, it's better to identify and discuss several possible solutions. Here's an important principle: The *more solutions you can identify, the greater the chance that you'll find one that is mutually acceptable.* The fewer solutions that you consider, the less likely it is that you'll be able to reach an agreement that everyone supports. One of the best strategies to generating possible solutions is to brainstorm for ideas.

To use brainstorming, consider the following suggestions:

1. Make sure the problem and the goals are clear to both of you.

2. When generating possible solutions, don't evaluate the solutions.

3. Try to come up with as many potential solutions as possible during a specifically allotted period of time.

4. Consider having each partner brainstorm ideas separately before a meeting, or write ideas down on paper before sharing the solutions with one another. Some people can think better when they write than when they speak.

5. Don't censor your ideas; try to develop at least one unique or wild idea. You can always tame wild ideas down later.

6. Piggyback off the ideas of your partner. Encourage your partner to use or modify your ideas.

7. Capture all ideas in writing. Write them down so that you don't lose any possible solutions. We tend to remember what we say first and last; you might come up with good ideas in the middle of your discussion but if you don't write them down you may not remember them.

8. After you've generated the ideas, then review the list; note ways to combine, eliminate, or extend the ideas.

The goal of brainstorming should be to come up with as many potential solutions as possible rather than try to find the one best idea. *The key to making brainstorming work is to separate the generation of ideas from the evaluation of ideas.* If you start evaluating ideas as they are suggested you're likely to limit the number of ideas you generate.

Select the Best **S**olution

The last step in the process (and the last "S" in the PUGSS acronym) is to select the best *solution* that you've identified. How do you do that? Determine which of the solutions that you've identified best helps you and your partner achieve your goals. Look at your list of possible solutions and evaluate them based upon your goals and criteria. As your textbook suggests, you are more likely to manage the conflict if you base your decisions on objective criteria. Criteria are the standards of an acceptable solution. For example, sample criteria might include the following: The solution should be agreeable to both parties; it should be able to be implemented within one week, and whatever solution is devised it should not cost more than fifty dollars. Identifying your criteria is important because it lets you know when you've reached a mutually agreeable solution.

If after considerable discussion you are not able to arrive at a mutually acceptable solution, you may decide to keep at it. Or you may decide that you need some help to sort out the issues, in which case you could take your problem to an impartial person who can help you identify conflict management strategies and solutions. If the conflict is at work, your immediate supervisors may be able to help. Or, if the conflict is so intractable, you may decide to agree to disagree rather than continuing to search for a mutually acceptable solution.

Don't get the idea that *all* conflict can be resolved by using the PUGSS formula. Managing differences is an art rather than an exact science. Conflict management rarely follows a linear, step-by-step sequence of events. These skill steps are designed to serve as a general framework for managing differences. The PUGSS approach works best if both you and your partner seek a collaborative approach to managing conflict. And in reality you don't simply describe the problem, achieve understanding, clearly define goals, and then generate and find the ideal solution. Sorting out your goals and your partner's goals is not typically something you do once and then put behind you. In reality, it will take time and patience to achieve your goals as well as your partner's goals. Nonetheless, the PUGSS approach does offer a framework to help you sort through problems and issues that create conflict. Think of these conflict management skills as options to consider, rather than as hard-and-fast rules to follow in every situation.

RECAP: PUGSS

A Structured Plan for Using Conflict Management Skills

P U G S S

Problem

> **Describe It**
> - Manage emotions by selecting a mutually acceptable time and place to discuss a conflict
> - Use "I" messages
> - Plan your message
> - Monitor nonverbal messages
> - Avoid personal attacks
> - Use self-talk to stay focused and to avoid letting your emotions escalate

Understanding

> **Achieve It**
> - Use effective listening skills while using "I" messages
> - Check your understanding of what others say and do: Paraphrase appropriately
> - Don't move on in sorting out the conflict until all parties understand one another

Goals

> **Identify Them**
> - Identify your goal in the conflict
> - Identify your partner's goal in the conflict
> - Identify where your goals and your partner's goals overlap

Solutions

> **Brainstorm**
> - Generate many possible solutions
> - Separate the evaluation of ideas from the generation of ideas
> - Piggyback off the ideas of your partner
> - Write down all possible solutions

Solution

> **Select the Best One**
> - Review the goals of each person
> - Select the solution that best achieves the goals

Interpersonal Conflict—PUGSS
PUGSS Role Play Activity
Directions:

You and your partner will be enacting this role-play for members of your class. You will construct your conversation using the PUGSS model for managing conflict. Please make sure that you acknowledge each step in the PUGSS process during your conversation. After each dyad presents, as a class answer the following questions:

1. What is the problem? What is the conflict?
2. Who is involved? What is their relationship? Are the people involved interdependent? What do the people in the scenario want? What is the ultimate goal?
3. What are some potential solutions to the problem? (Brainstorming) Which solution do you recommend, and why?

Possible Scenarios:

You and your roommate have been friends since high school, and you just moved into your first apartment. Your roommate is interested in having parties and inviting people over all the time, while you do not. You tried to be flexible, but you finally felt the need to say something when he/she threw a party the night before your big mid-term exam.

You and your best friend are interested in dating the same person. You each met this person separately, so neither knew you were interested in the same person. You found out when you were all at the same party together. Now, you are trying to figure out whether or not either of you should keep seeing the person or if you should just leave him/her alone.

You have been dating someone for the last 6 months when suddenly, he/she begins to change. You see a significant change in the amount of time he/she spends working out, eating healthy, and being worried about his/her looks. You begin to feel as though you don't want to date someone who is consumed by this, so you decide to sit down and talk about it.

One of your siblings has been dating someone for a few years. Unfortunately, you do not care for this person, and he/she is always rude to you. You feel as though your brother/sister will be getting engaged soon, and you want to have a conversation about your concerns before this happens.

Your roommate is upset that you have not been picking up and your apartment is a complete mess. You find out that your roommate has been talking to other people about what is bothering him/her about your living situation. Instead of discussing the issue with you, he/she spoke to some of the other people living in your dorm. In fact, you had no idea anything was bothering him/her until the other people told you about it. Now, you are upset and decide to confront him/her.

You have been living with your significant other for a year. You are beginning to feel very frustrated that you work all day, go to school, and then come home to a messy house. You begin to distance yourself from your relational partner rather than argue about the mess. Now, your boy/girlfriend confronts you about why you have been so distant.

Your roommate likes to spend time with you—unfortunately, you feel like he/she is spending too much time with you. He/she is hanging out with your friends and constantly is around. You begin to feel suffocated and want some space.

You have been sick and finally figured out you have mono. You have been missing classes, and now you are failing because of your absences and missing assignments. In order to get a passing grade in the class, you have to ask for some leniency from your professor. You want to be able to make up any missing work, but your professor is reluctant because you did not communicate and let him/her know what was going on.

Your boss consistently gives exciting and innovating projects to one of your co-workers. You begin to feel as though you are not valued as a member of the team. In fact, you start to believe that your boss is discriminating against you (because of your race/sexual orientation/gender/age). You decide that it is time to confront your boss to figure out what is going on.

You bought a DVD player at Target, but when you tried to play a DVD, it did not work. You lost your receipt and now are trying to return it to Target. Unfortunately, Target does not accept items without receipts.

One of your co-workers has been consistently arriving to work late. Your boss has not noticed and has not said anything to your co-worker. You are beginning to become frustrated that he/she is getting away with being late. You decide to confront your coworker.

You are having a gathering at your new house. Without asking, someone lights up a cigarette in the house. You are completely offended and try to talk to the other person. Unfortunately, the other person doesn't feel like it is a problem.

Your spouse consistently comes home late from work. Although your spouse always says he/she will be home early, somehow he/she ends up missing dinner and for the last week, you have eaten dinner by yourself.

Your boss needs a report for an 8 AM meeting tomorrow morning and asks you to stay late to finish it. Unfortunately, you already have a meeting scheduled for after work and won't be able to complete the report tonight. You want to explain to your boss why you will not be able to complete the task.

You have just received your credit card bill and you find charges for purchases you never made. You contact your customer service representative, but find out that the credit card company doesn't offer fraud protection, so they want you to pay for all of the charges.

Putnam & Wilson Conflict Style Scale

Think of conflicts you have encountered with other people you care about. Indicate below how frequently you engage in each of the described behaviors. For each item, select the number that represents the behavior you are most likely to exhibit. There are no right or wrong answers. Please respond to all items on the scale. The responses are as follows: 1 = Very Seldom; 2 = Seldom; 3 = Sometimes; 4 = Often; 5 = Very Often.

_____ 1. I shy away from topics that are the source of disputes.

_____ 2. I insist that my position be accepted during a conflict.

_____ 3. I suggest solutions that combine a variety of viewpoints.

_____ 4. I steer clear of disagreeable situations.

_____ 5. I raise my voice when trying to get another person to accept my position.

_____ 6. I keep quiet about my views in order to avoid disagreements.

_____ 7. I frequently give a little if the other person will meet me halfway.

_____ 8. I meet the opposition at the midpoint of our differences.

_____ 9. I assert my opinion forcefully.

_____ 10. I dominate arguments until the other person understands my position.

_____ 11. I suggest we work together to create solutions to disagreements.

_____ 12. I try to use everyone's ideas to generate solutions to problems.

_____ 13. I argue insistently for my stance.

_____ 14. I sidestep disagreements when they arise.

_____ 15. I stand firm in my views during a conflict.

_____ 16. I avoid a person I suspect of wanting to discuss a disagreement.

_____ 17. I will go fifty-fifty to reach a settlement.

_____ 18. I ease conflict by claiming our differences are trivial.

INSTRUCTIONS FOR SCORING:

The 18 scale items measure three types of conflict styles: nonconfrontation oriented, cooperative oriented, and confrontational oriented. In the spaces below, record the number you answered for each item. Sum the column and compare your total to the standards shown.

Interpersonal Conflict Styles

Nonconfrontation	Cooperative	Confrontational
1.	3.	2.
4.	7.	5.
6.	8.	9.
14.	11.	10.
16.	12.	13.
18.	17.	15.
Total:	Total:	Total:

Conflict Style Descriptions

Nonconfrontation Style: Indirect strategies for handling a conflict; choosing to avoid or withdraw from a disagreement; such communicative behaviors as silence, glossing over differences, and concealing ill feelings.

Cooperative Style: Direct communication about the conflict; behaviors that aim to find a solution, to integrate the needs of both parties, and to give in or compromise on issues.

Confrontational Style: Direct communication about the disagreement, arguing persistently for one's position, taking control of the interaction, and advocating one's position.

STANDARDS:

Total 6–9   = Very Seldom
Total 10–15 = Seldom
Total 16–21 = Sometimes
Total 22–27 = Often
Total 28–30 = Very Often

Adapted From:

Putnam, L. L., & Wilson, C. E. (1982). Communicative strategies and organizational conflicts: Reliability and validity of a measurement scale. *Communication Yearbook, 6,* 629–652.

Study Guide for Communicating in the Interpersonal Context Module

Chapter 7 Understanding Interpersonal Communication

1. Be able to **differentiate** interpersonal and impersonal communication.

2. Be able to **differentiate** the following factors of interpersonal attraction: similarity, physical attraction, sexual attraction, proximity, and complementarity.

3. Be able to **identify** communication strategies that passively, actively, and interactively reduce uncertainty.

4. Be able to **explain** the role of reciprocity and appropriateness in self-disclosure.

5. Be able to **identify** two aspects of the social penetration model of self-disclosure and **explain**, using the model, how self-disclosure moves a relationship toward intimacy.

6. Be able to **explain** the four quadrants of the Johari Window and know what each one represents.

Chapter 8 Enhancing Relationships

1. Be able to **identify** and **explain** each of the five relational escalation stages—pre-interaction awareness stage, initiation stage, exploration stage, intensification stage, and intimacy stage—and note how the five principles apply to each stage.

2. Be able to **identify** and **explain** each of the six relational de-escalation stages: turmoil or stagnation stage, de-intensification stage, individualization stage, separation stage, and post-interaction stage.

3. Be able to **identify** and **differentiate** nonconfrontational, confrontational, and cooperative conflict management styles.

4. Be able to **differentiate** between the three relational dialectics.

5. Be able to **differentiate** between the types of conflict.

PUGSS: Structuring Conflict Management Skills

1. Be able to **identify** the five stages of the PUGSS conflict management model. (Student Guidebook, Module Two).

2. Be able to **identify** the following communication behaviors in the PUGSS model: Descriptive versus Evaluative Language, Self-Disclosing Emotions, Perception Checking, Paraphrasing, Nonverbal Responsiveness, and Adapting. (Student Guidebook, Module Two).

3. Be able to **identify** and **describe** the five components of interpersonal conflict: expressed struggle, perceived incompatible goals, perceived scarce rewards/resources, interdependence, and climate of competition.

Sample Exam Questions
Module: Communicating in
the Interpersonal Context

Chapter 7   Understanding Interpersonal Communication

1. Melvin is driving on a long trip across the country when he pulls into a gas station. The gas attendant asks, "May I help you?" Melvin then replies, "I need 20 dollar's worth." According to the text what form of communication would this be considered?
    A. Impersonal communication
    B. Interpersonal communication
    C. Intrapersonal communication
    D. Interrelational communication

2. According to the Social Penetration Model, as breadth and depth of self-disclosure _____, intimacy _____.
    A. Increase, decreases
    B. Decrease, increases
    C. Increase, remains constant
    D. Increase, increases

3. According to Altman and Taylor's model of self-disclosure, partners' communication at the very intimate level has:
    A. Breadth, but not depth
    B. Depth, but not breadth
    C. Both breadth and depth
    D. Neither breadth nor depth

4. Maggie hugs her friends often and asks for hugs from them. She has a high need for:
    A. Inclusion
    B. Attraction
    C. Control
    D. Affection

5. Gary needs to talk to his professor about an assignment but he does not know how to get to her office. When he asks the professor for directions, Gary is engaging in which strategy of uncertainty reduction?
    A. Interactive
    B. Passive
    C. Active
    D. Intermediate

Chapter 8   Enhancing Relationships

1. During an initial conversation, Joel and Linda share basic information about themselves to determine what they have in common. Joel and Linda are in which stage of relational escalation?

    A. Pre-interaction awareness
    B. Initiation
    C. Exploration
    D. Intensification

2. Jennifer and Allison used to spend a lot of time together as roommates. Unfortunately, however, they are getting on each other's nerves and are experiencing more conflicts when they see each other. They both now are beginning to find

ways to avoid the other in order to keep peace in the house. Which stage of relational de-escalation are Jennifer and Allison experiencing?

A. Individualization X
B. Separation
C. De-intensification
D. Post-interaction X

3. Matthew was consistently feeling suffocated by his roommate, Kyle. Kyle, on the other hand, was feeling frustrated that Matthew wouldn't include him when he would go out with his friends. This is an example of which relational dialectic tension?

A. Real vs. ideal
B. Openness vs. closedness
C. Novelty vs. predictability
D. Autonomy vs. connection

4. George is approached by his roommate regarding a disagreement. His roommate complains about George's share of the bills that are piling up. Rather than get involved in a potentially hurtful argument, George leaves the room when the dialogue gets heated. George uses what kind of conflict style?

A. Cooperative
B. Confrontational
C. Nonconfrontational
D. Aggressive

5. When Tim walked into his house from a long vacation and saw clothes everywhere and the dishes piled up, he approached his roommate and said, "I noticed several articles of clothing on the floor and dishes in the kitchen. It seems that you have been either preoccupied or unaware of the mess in the house. Can you tell me what is going on?" This is an example of what communication behavior?

A. Adapting
B. Paraphrasing
C. Self-disclosing
D. Perception checking

PUGSS Structuring Conflict Management Skills

1. When Kerri told Lindsey, "You know, it's in both our best interest for you not to move out of our apartment and break our lease," she was engaging in which stage of PUGSS?

A. Describing the problem
B. Identifying individual and common goals
C. Brainstorming solutions
D. Achieving understanding

2. As Mark and Gina discussed the family feud over their wedding plans, Mark suggested they elope to Las Vegas. Gina thought it would be fun to get married before a justice of the peace. Then Mark added that getting married on a Caribbean cruise with the closest family members might be exciting. The PUGSS stage in which Mark and Gina were interacting was:

A. Identifying goals
B. Achieving mutual understanding
C. Describing the problem
D. Brainstorming possible solutions

3. Which one of the following is NOT an underlying principle for the Cooperative Style of Conflict?
    A. Separate people from the problem
    B. Focus on shared interests
    C. Base decisions on objective criterion
    D. Agree to accept positive solutions

Answer Key

CHAPTER 7

1. A
2. D
3. C
4. D
5. A

CHAPTER 8

1. B
2. C

3. D
4. C
5. D

PUGSS

1. B
2. D
3. D

MODULE 3
COMMUNICATING IN THE INFORMATIVE SPEAKING CONTEXT

After completing this module (Chapters 11, 12, and 14), you will be able to:

PRINCIPLE 1
Be aware of your communication with yourself and others.

- Identify strategies for enhancing your self-confidence when speaking before audiences.
- Manage your own presentational speaking apprehension.
- Understand how audience members perceive you and how these perceptions influence whether they find you and your message credible.

PRINCIPLE 2
Effectively use and interpret verbal messages.

- Identify the differences between informative and persuasive messages.
- Narrow speech topic appropriately and develop thesis/propositional statement that meets the objective or purpose of the public presentation.
- Identify and use appropriate organizational pattern for speaker purpose and audience needs: chronological, spatial, topical, problem–solution, or motivated sequence.
- Identify and use appropriate forms of supporting material: definitions, detailed descriptions, analogies, anecdotes, examples, statistical information, quotation, and testimony.
- Identify and use language that remains appropriate for audience, purpose, and situation.
- Identify and use fundamental principles of verbal clarity.
- Identify and use appropriate introductions and conclusions.
- Understand and use fundamental principles of outlining.

- Orally cite sources in presentations.
- Identify and use verbal messages to enhance credibility.
- Identify and use verbal messages that evoke appropriate emotions.

PRINCIPLE 3
Effectively use and interpret nonverbal messages.

- Effectively deliver presentation using appropriate nonverbal behaviors: eye contact, posture, kinesic behavior (bodily movement and gestures), and vocalic behavior (rate, volume, variety, pitch, articulation, and nonvocalized pauses).
- Monitor audience nonverbal feedback and make necessary adjustments to adapt to audience needs.

PRINCIPLE 4
Listen and respond thoughtfully to others.

- Critically evaluate speaker credibility, as an audience member.
- Critically evaluate the organization of the speaker's argument.
- Critically evaluate the speaker's supporting material and/or evidence.

PRINCIPLE 5
Appropriately adapt messages to others.

- Analyze audience, paying particular attention to audience characteristics (race, ethnicity, sex, age, attitudes, beliefs, values) and ethically adapt or modify message to achieve presentation goal.
- Analyze situation or occasion, paying particular attention to time, place, and audience expectation, and ethically adapt or modify message to achieve presentation goal.
- Identify and use the appropriate style of delivery for the audience, situation, and purpose: manuscript, memorization, extemporaneous, and impromptu.

Chapter 11
Lecture Notes

Chapter 12
Lecture Notes

Chapter 14
Lecture Notes

Audience-Centered Speaking Model

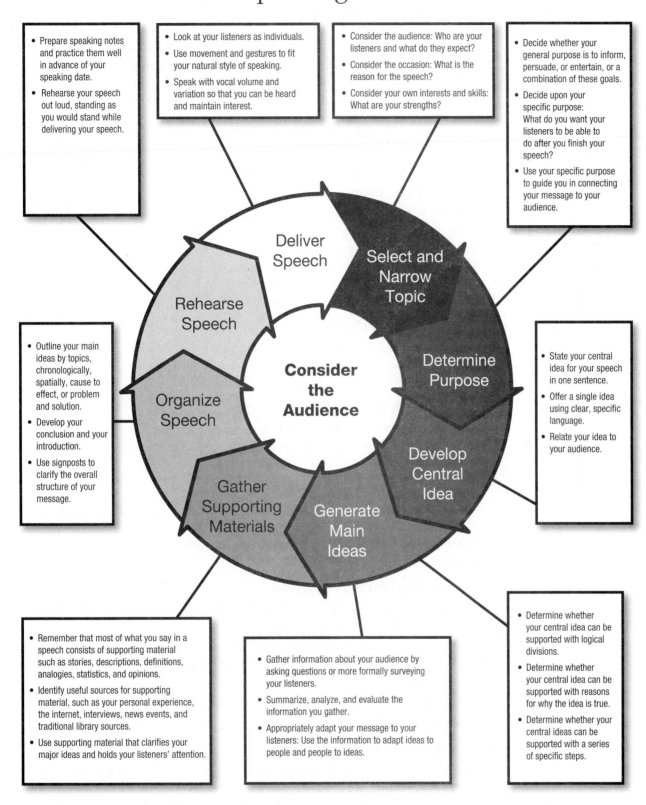

- Prepare speaking notes and practice them well in advance of your speaking date.
- Rehearse your speech out loud, standing as you would stand while delivering your speech.

- Look at your listeners as individuals.
- Use movement and gestures to fit your natural style of speaking.
- Speak with vocal volume and variation so that you can be heard and maintain interest.

- Consider the audience: Who are your listeners and what do they expect?
- Consider the occasion: What is the reason for the speech?
- Consider your own interests and skills: What are your strengths?

- Decide whether your general purpose is to inform, persuade, or entertain, or a combination of these goals.
- Decide upon your specific purpose: What do you want your listeners to be able to do after you finish your speech?
- Use your specific purpose to guide you in connecting your message to your audience.

- Outline your main ideas by topics, chronologically, spatially, cause to effect, or problem and solution.
- Develop your conclusion and your introduction.
- Use signposts to clarify the overall structure of your message.

- State your central idea for your speech in one sentence.
- Offer a single idea using clear, specific language.
- Relate your idea to your audience.

- Remember that most of what you say in a speech consists of supporting material such as stories, descriptions, definitions, analogies, statistics, and opinions.
- Identify useful sources for supporting material, such as your personal experience, the internet, interviews, news events, and traditional library sources.
- Use supporting material that clarifies your major ideas and holds your listeners' attention.

- Gather information about your audience by asking questions or more formally surveying your listeners.
- Summarize, analyze, and evaluate the information you gather.
- Appropriately adapt your message to your listeners: Use the information to adapt ideas to people and people to ideas.

- Determine whether your central idea can be supported with logical divisions.
- Determine whether your central idea can be supported with reasons for why the idea is true.
- Determine whether your central ideas can be supported with a series of specific steps.

Circle labels: Deliver Speech · Select and Narrow Topic · Rehearse Speech · Determine Purpose · Consider the Audience · Organize Speech · Develop Central Idea · Gather Supporting Materials · Generate Main Ideas

Source: Fig 2.3 p. 32 Public Speaking, 10/e Steven A. Beebe 0134380916

Sample Reference Page Citations in APA Format

The outline you hand in to your lab instructor before you begin speaking must include a bibliography of at least three published sources used in the speech. The source citations in the bibliography must conform to APA style. These are sample citations for the most common types of sources you might use in completing the two speech assignments in the form required by the most recent edition of the *Publication Manual of the American Psychological Association, 6th Edition.* That handbook is available at all bookstores and in the Alkek Library. Please consult the handbook for the proper citation form for types of sources not listed here.

AN ARTICLE IN A SCHOLARLY JOURNAL

Author's Name: Last name first, followed by initials. (Publication date). Title of article. Title of journal, (italicized), volume number (italicized), page numbers. Doi (no period at end of reference)

Mottet, T. P. (2000). Interactive television instructors' perceptions of students' nonverbal responsiveness and their influence on distance teaching. *Communication Education, 49,* 146–164. doi:10.1080/03634520009379202

AN ARTICLE IN A MAGAZINE

Author's name: Last name first, followed by initials. (Publication date). Title of article. Title of magazine (italicized), volume (italicized), page numbers.

Meyer, A. S., (1995, October). Antibiotic resistance. *Time, 9,* 47–54.

AN ARTICLE IN A NEWSPAPER, NO AUTHOR

Title of article. (Publication date). Title of newspaper (italicized), page number.

New drug appears to sharply cut risk of death from heart failure. (1993, July 15). *The Washington Post,* p. A12.

A BOOK WITH A SINGLE AUTHOR PUBLICATION

Author's Name: Last name first, followed by initials. (Publication date). Title of book (italicized). Place of publication: Publisher.

Mehrabian, A. (1971). *Silent messages.* Belmont, CA: Wadsworth Publishing Company, Inc.

A BOOK WITH MULTIPLE AUTHORS

Authors' names: Last name first, followed by initials. (Publication date). Title of book (italicized). Place of publication: Publisher.

Burgoon, J. K., Stern, L. A., & Dillman, L. (1995). *Interpersonal adaptation: Dyadic interaction patterns.* New York: Cambridge University Press.

References to Online Information

Please reference "Electronic Media" in the *APA Publication Manual (6th ed.).*

AN ARTICLE IN NEWSPAPER, NO AUTHOR

Title of online article. (Publication date). Title of periodical (italicized). Retrieved from http://Web address (no period at end of reference)

New drug appears to sharply cut risk of death from heart failure. (1993, July 15). *The Washington Post.* Retrieved from http://www.washingtonpost.com/featurearticle.html

AN ONLINE ARTICLE PUBLISHED IN A SCHOLARLY JOURNAL

Authors' Names: Last name first, followed by initials. (Publication date). Title of article. Title of journal (italicized), volume number, page numbers. Doi (no period at end of reference)

McCroskey, J. C., & Andersen, J. F. (1976). The relationship between communication apprehension and academic achievement among college students. *Human Communication Research, 5, 3–81.* doi: 10.1037/0021-9010.76.1.143

AN ONLINE MAGAZINE ARTICLE

Author's Name: Last name first, followed by initials. (Publication date). Title of article. Title of magazine (italicized), page numbers. Retrieved from http://Web address (no period at end of reference)

Meyer, A. S. (1995, October 29). Antibiotic resistance. *Time,* 47–54. Retrieved from http://www.ccm.Isumc.edu/bugbytes/Volume2/bb-v2n13.html

NONPERIODICAL WEB DOCUMENT, WEB PAGE, OR REPORT

Author's Name: Last name first, followed by initials. (Publication date). Title of document. Retrieved from http://Web address (no period at end of reference)

Angeli, E., Wagner, J., Lawrick, E., Moore, K., Anderson, M., Soderland, L., & Brizee, A. (2010, May 5). General format. Retrieved from http://owl.english.purdue.edu/owl/resource/560/01/

Checklist for Evaluating Information Found on the Internet

Ask Yourself Five Important Questions

Did I identify the source?

Who is providing the information?

❑ Is the author mentioned in a positive fashion by another author or another person I trust as an authority?

❑ Did I find or link to the author's Web/internet document from another document I trust?

❑ Does the Web/internet document I am reading provide me with biographical information, including the author's position, institutional affiliation, and address?

❑ Is the biographical information available by linking to another document? (This enables you to judge whether the author's credentials allow him/her to speak with authority on a given topic.)

❑ If none of the above exists, is there an address and telephone number as well as an e-mail address for the author in order to request further information on his/her work and professional background? (An e-mail address alone gives you no more information than you already have.)

Did I discover the source's expertise?

Is the source an expert or authority?

❑ Did I examine credentials in the author's bios and "about us" pages?

❑ Did I check the grammar and spelling for accuracy?

❑ Did I examine links to and from other Web sites?

❑ Did I look for other publications by the author or publisher? (Check Amazon.com)

❑ Did I independently verify credentials?

◊ Did I verify college degrees? (Call registrar's office.)

◊ Did I verify the professional associations? (Check professional directory)

◊ Is the person cited as an expert in the news or trade literature?

◊ Has the person published articles in trade literature or peer-reviewed publications?

Did I determine the level of objectivity?

Does the source provide a balanced viewpoint?

❑ Did I examine the writing style? Is it trying to influence my opinion?

❑ Did I examine the advertising? Does it influence the content?

❑ Note: Lack of objectivity does not necessarily mean the source provides substandard information. A persuasive writer intends to win your favor. He/she might use good facts and analyses to do so.

❑ Note the URL of the document. Does this document reside on the Web server of an organization that has a clear stake in the issue at hand? If you are looking at a corporate Web site, assume that the information on the corporation will present it in the most positive light. If you are looking at products produced and sold by that corporation, remember that you are looking at an advertisement. If you are reading about a political figure on the Web site of another political party, you are reading the opposition.

❑ Does this document reside on the Web server of an organization that has a political or philosophical agenda? If you are looking for scientific information on human genetics, would you trust a political or religious organization to provide it? Never assume that extremist points of view are always easy to detect. Some sites promoting these views may look educational.

Did I establish the date of publication?

Is the information current at the time of publication? Did I examine creation and revision dates? (Do not rely on dates provided by search engines.)

❑ Did I review facts and analyses in historical context?

❑ Did I assess the writing for time-sensitive information? (Be cautious about descriptive words such as *always, never, all, none,* and *most.*)

❑ Does the document include the date(s) at which the information was gathered (e.g., U.S. Census data)?

❑ Does the document refer to clearly dated information (e.g., "Based on 1990 U.S. Census data.")?

❑ Where there is a need to add data or update it on a constant basis, does the document include information on the regularity of updates?

❑ Does the document include a publication date or a "last updated" date?

❑ Does the document include a date of copyright?

❑ If no date is given in an electronic document, can I view the directory in which it resides and read the date of the latest modification?

Did I verify what the information claims?

Can I find two or more reliable sources that provide the same information?

❑ Did I use primary sources (sources that originate information) for facts?

❑ Did I use secondary sources (sources that interpret facts), and do the secondary sources provide cited references?

❑ Did I look for cited references?

This information was adapted from The Sheridan Libraries at Johns Hopkins University Web site: http://www.library .jhu.edu/researchhelp/general/evaluating/

A special thanks to Trish Bode for recommending this information.

Suggestions for Rehearsing Your Presentation

The objective of this lab is to give you the opportunity to practice speaking in an instructional environment that is free from evaluation. During this lab you will present, in an extemporaneous manner, a 3-minute briefing where you inform your audience of the problem you will be examining in your problem–solution persuasive presentation.

Following each briefing, your lab instructors and classmates will provide you with immediate constructive feedback. This feedback will focus on information that was unclear and strategies for how you can adapt your message to the audience to enhance clarity and understanding.

The informative briefing must meet the following criteria:

1. Briefings must be 2 to 3 minutes in length.

2. Briefings must be delivered in an extemporaneous style.

3. Include one published source that is orally cited and made credible. (How to make oral attributions will be discussed later in this module guide.)

4. Include a thesis statement. "In the next 3 minutes, I would like to brief you on the problem of _____."

5. The informative briefings must answer the following three questions:

- What is the problem? This needs to be descriptive and should address some of the following: Who? What? Where? When? How? Why?
- How does the problem affect the audience? Address issues of relevance.
- How do we know that it's a problem? What evidence is there that supports your claim that the problem actually exists? Sample evidence includes quotes, statistics, expert and/or personal testimony, anecdotes, etc.

- Practicing or rehearsing your presentations before you deliver them in class is absolutely essential. Exactly how you practice and how many times will vary from person to person. Usually, speakers should practice out loud, standing up, three to six times before delivering the presentation to the audience. But regardless of how and how many times you rehearse, here are some tips that can help:
- As you rehearse, listen for language problems such as jargon or slang that may not be appropriate for your audience.
- Exaggerate your nonverbal gestures while practicing your presentation. You will find that they will soon become natural.
- Practice your eye contact. Pretend that the audience is in front of you. Practice your eye contact by moving your eyes naturally around the room.
- Time your presentation during rehearsal. Remember to time your presentation every time you practice because adjustments to presentations will alter timing. Remember also that you may tend to talk faster in front of the audience. Allow for that.
- Allow time for adjustments. While practicing, you are also polishing your presentation, so start practicing early.
- Never write the presentation out word for word and then either read it aloud or memorize it. You must use extemporaneous delivery for both presentations in this class.
- Practice pauses. You may want to indicate on your notes cards where pauses are appropriate. The more familiar you are with your presentation, the more evident the places for pauses will become.

- You may want to shift your position for the main points. That is, some speakers will move to the right for the first point, center for second, and left for third. Most introductions and conclusions are presented in center positions. If you decide to do this in your presentations, practice the movements.
- Give yourself a dress rehearsal. This will allow you to adjust your choices of clothing if necessary. You are more confident of yourself when you feel like you look good.
- Beware of "uhs," "ums," "you knows," "likes," "ehrs," and "whatevers."

Following those suggestions will not guarantee that you will give an outstanding presentation. But failing to follow them will almost guarantee that you will give a bad one!

Managing Presentational Speaking Apprehension

BEFORE SPEECH DAY

- Prepare well. It is harder to be confident if you do not have good content that you are familiar with.
- Practice.

  Practice out loud!!!

  Practice while looking at a picture of students in a classroom. Use your note-cards, not your outline, to practice.

SPEECH DAY – BEFORE CLASS

- Exercise. A brisk walk will help.
- Dress well so you feel good about yourself.

SPEECH DAY – DURING CLASS

- Focus on telling the audience what you want them to know, not on how you will look, feel, etc.
- Take slow deep breaths if you start to feel anxious.
- Concentrate on the other speeches.
- Use mind games. Tell yourself you will do great; tell yourself you want your audience to know what you are telling them; interpret the feelings of anxiety as excitement, not fear; tell yourself you can do it—because you can and you will.

ADDITIONAL TIPS

Sometimes the adrenaline just makes crazy things happen, so to hide some of those things:

- For shaking: Don't keep your hands in one place. Put your note cards down and then pull them up again when you need them.
- For red spotting: Wear a shirt with a high neckline. It will take longer for it to be noticeable, and may not be at all.
- For sweating: Wear a loose, light-colored shirt.

COMM Lab: Getting Started

How Do I Make an Appointment for the COMM Lab?

- Type "COMM Lab" into the University search engine.
- Click the link.
- Read all information on the website.
- Scroll down to the calendar and click the time slot you want.
- Fill in the requested information and submit.
- Check your Texas State e-mail for confirmation.
- **Appointments fill up fast, so please make yours ASAP.**

Where Is COMM Lab?

- The Lab is located on the fourth floor of Alkek Library, **Room 480A.**

What if I Cannot Make My Appointment?

- If you can't attend your appointment, **it is very important that you cancel your appointment at least 24 hours in advance.**
- How to cancel your appointment:
    - Check the confirmation e-mail you received.
    - Find **"To cancel this booking, click this link."**
    - Click the link and follow the instructions.
- Please do not "No Show." **If you do not cancel your appointment and fail to show up at your designated time, your presentation score will be deducted 5 points.** Your instructor will be notified if you do not make your appointment.

How Should I Prepare for My COMM Lab Appointment?

- Practice your presentation, roleplay, etc. *before* you come to the Lab.
- Staff members are trained to assist with *delivery* aspects.

What Will Happen in COMM Lab?

- You will deliver your presentation to an experienced staff member.
- Your performance will be recorded.
- After performing, you will observe the presentation with the staff member and receive a critique.
- The staff member will provide a written copy of your feedback.

Can I Get a Copy of My Presentation?

- We will e-mail you a link to your video.

Informative Presentation Assignment

Assignment Rationale

A survey of human resource managers revealed that oral communication (specifically speaking skills) remains the number one factor in helping graduating college students obtain employment. Additionally, a recent survey of both communication teachers and students found that the single most important skill taught in a communication course is how to give an informative presentation. This assignment allows you to integrate the five principles of human communication into your own informative presentation.

General Learning Objectives

Upon completing this assignment, you will be able to do the following:

1. Select and narrow a topic for an informative presentation about objects, people, events, or ideas.

2. Create a preview statement with three main points.

3. Develop an informative presentation that is adapted to your audience.

4. Outline an informative presentation using an Introduction, Body, and Conclusion.

5. Support your presentation using appropriate support material and cite sources orally.

6. Use precise, clear, and descriptive language.

7. Deliver an informative presentation in an extemporaneous manner using appropriate nonverbal behaviors: eye contact, bodily movement, gestures, and vocal variety.

Assignment Expectations

In order to complete this assignment, you will be expected to complete thse steps:

1. Develop, organize, adapt, and present a 5- to 7-minute informative presentation.

2. Complete the Topic Selection worksheet and obtain topic approval from your instructor.

3. Complete a Preparation Outline (using proper outline format), and a bibliography with Audience Adaptation Plan and **Turnitin** Originality Report.

4. Develop speaking notes that reflect your instructor's feedback from the preparation outline.

NOTE: Be on time and ready to present on your assigned day. As speeches run on a tight schedule, if you miss your speaking time/day, you may not have an opportunity to make it up and will be counted absent.

Principles Targeted

1. **Be aware of your communication with yourself and others:** This assignment will challenge you to become more aware of how you communicate in public speaking encounters. Pay close attention to your idiosyncrasies when you experience communication apprehension.

2. **Effectively use and interpret verbal messages:** This assignment will require you to develop effective and organized content in a 5- to 7-minute presentation that will focus on an informative speech topic.

3. **Effectively use and interpret nonverbal messages:** This assignment will require you to use effective nonverbal delivery including vocal variety, eye contact, appropriate body movement, and gestures during your presentation.

4. **Listen and respond thoughtfully to others:** This assignment will challenge you to listen thoughtfully and actively as an audience member during the presentations.

5. **Appropriately adapt your messages to others:** This assignment will require you to adapt your messages to your audience while preparing for and delivering your oral presentation.

Informative Presentation - Items Due on Speech Day

1. Informative Presentation Assessment Form – Turn in blank (Guidebook) Pg. 127

2. Informative Presentation Speaking Notes (should look like sample outlines in Pg Guidebook)

3. Informative Presentation Speaking Notes Assessment Form – Turn in blank Pg 125 (Guidebook)

4. Completed Informative Audience Adaptation Plan (Guidebook) Pg 111

5. BOTH Audience Member Assessment Forms (2 identical sheets, Guidebook) Pg 129 & 131

NOTE: THESE DOCUMENTS SHOULD BE TURNED IN, IN YOUR MANILA FOLDERS AND IN ORDER IMMEDIATELY BEFORE YOU PRESENT.

SUGGESTIONS FOR CITING SOURCES ORALLY Each time supporting material from one of your sources is used in a speech, whether you quote the source directly or simply paraphrase what the source said, that supporting material must be orally attributed to its source. A cited source is not a full bibliographic citation. Rather, it is a shortened form of the bibliographic citation that nevertheless lets your listeners know where the supporting material came from. Following are some examples:

- At a minimum you must state the name of the source. For example, "According to Helen Warren ..." or "As *Psychology Today* reported ..."

- Sometimes it is also important to explain the qualifications of your source. That is especially true if your listeners are unfamiliar with that source. For example, "According to Helen Warren, Associate Professor of Abnormal Psychology at Harvard University ..."

- It might also be necessary to provide the date of publication. This is especially true when dealing with a topic of current importance that changes rapidly. For example, "The August 14, 2005, issue of *Psychology Today* reported ..."

- And sometimes it may be necessary to provide an even more complete attribution. That might be the case when an issue is especially controversial and differences of opinion are common. For example, "According to Helen Warren, Associate Professor of Abnormal Psychology at Harvard University, writing in the August 14, 2005, issue of *Psychology Today* ..."

In any case, whenever supporting material from your sources is used in the speech, whether that material is quoted directly or simply paraphrased, you must attribute that material orally to its source.

Informative Speech Topics

Remember, informative presentations are often about objects, people, procedures, events, or ideas. If your speech is a "problem–solution" speech, then you need to re-work your topic so that it is strictly informative. If you are struggling to come up with something, browse the list below to help you brainstorm.

SAMPLE TOPICS

Smart cars

Tuxedos

Saxophones

Green tea

Sickle cell anemia

How steel pan drums are made

Paulo Freire

How film is developed

Jane Elliot

Bipolar disorder

Marxism

Steampunk fashion

Types of espresso drinks

Maya Angelou

Toilets

Film noir

"Free running"

Mediterranean cuisine

Frisbee golf

The origins of hip-hop

Milton Glaser

The Libertarian Party

Informative Presentation Worksheet

Speaker's Name: _____

Worksheet Partner's Name: _____

Introduction

1. Discuss your attention-getter with your partner.

   A. What strategy are you using (story, statistics, quotes)?

   B. Do you and your partner believe it will be effective? If yes, how do you know this? If not, what will you do to make it more effective?

2. Discuss how you are establishing relevance and common ground with your audience throughout the presentation.

3. What is your initial preview statement? An initial preview statement previews the three main points of the speech so that the audience knows where you are going. If you don't have one, try developing one with your partner.

4. How will you establish credibility?

Body

5. What type(s) of evidence are you using in your presentation (magazines, newspaper, website)?

6. Are you prepared to cite ALL sources in your presentation? Do you have at least three published sources? Write out, in sentences, how you will orally cite all of your sources in the space below.

7. Does your partner believe your sources are valid and appropriate?

8. Does your outline reflect the use of precise, clear, and descriptive language? Write down, in the space below, two good language choices. Also, write down two language choices that need improvement.

9. What two things do you need to work on to improve the body of your speech?

   A.

   B.

10. Review your outline with your partner.

    A. Identify and correct formatting errors. Make sure the outline resembles the example found in the *Guidebook*.

    B. Are sources in the outline cited appropriately in APA format? References within the outline (not the bibliography) should be author and year (Jones, 2001).

    C. Did you use APA format for the references?

Delivery

11. Discuss your (planned/rehearsed) delivery.

    A. What do you think your strengths are in terms of delivery? (After seeing your outline and hearing you speak in class throughout the semester, what does your partner perceive your strengths to be?)

    B. What are you concerned about regarding your delivery?

    C. How will you cope/improve those concerns prior to your presentation?

    D. How do you believe your instructor and/or peers can help you through the presentation process?

Informative Speech Preparation Outline Assessment Form (15 pts)

Name: _____ Total Score: _____ /15

Topic: _____

Name of Instructor: _____

(**+ = Excellent ✔ = Fair — = Poor**)

---

3 Body Paragraphs

_____ Topic is narrow

_____ Topic is relevant to the audience

_____ Used proper outline format – Mirrors Guidebook examples

_____ Specific purpose indicated

_____ Central idea included

_____ Initial preview with main points included

_____ 3 well-developed body paragraphs with 1 source clearly cited in each

_____ 3 sources support topic

_____ Used descriptive and objective language

_____ Final summary indicated – Conclusion

_____ Transitions jndicated throughout

_____ Included reference page with 3 different sources using APA format

_____ Included **completed** Audience Adaptation Plan (Rated items and written responses included)

*NOTE: Students earning above 20% on their Turnitin Originality Reports will receive a ZERO on the preparation outline grade and will be required to resubmit their revised preparation outline (and demonstrate a plagiarism report score under 20%) before being allowed to present.

_____

_____

_____

Informative Audience Adaptation Plan

Student Name: _Megan Hawthorne_

Presentation Topic: _Diabetes_

SPECIFIC PRESENTATION GOAL: At the end of my presentation, my audience will *understand*:

This is what I know about my audience:

1. My audience's demographic profile includes:

   Sex: _____ Male _____ Female   Average Age: _19.8_   Ethnicities: _____

   Class Rank: _80%_ Fresh _____ Soph _____ Jr _____ Sr

   Group Memberships:

2. On a scale from 1 to 5 (1 = Low, 5 = High), how relevant and interesting is my initial preview statement to my audience?
   _4,4,3,4,5,5,5,5,4,5_

   Write your own preview statement here:
   differences & treatment of diabetes

3. On a scale from 1 to 5 (1 = Little, 5 = A lot), my audience's level of knowledge about my topic is _____.
   Explain why you believe their knowledge of your topic would be at this level.
   _2,2,3,4,4,4,4,3,3,2,4_

4. On a scale from 1 to 5 (1 = Little, 5 = A lot), my audience's perceptions of my credibility will be _____.
   Explain how you plan to establish your credibility with the audience.
   _1,2,3,4,5,5,4,4,4,4,4_

5. Based on this information, provide two examples here of how you will adapt your presentation to this audience.
   I will talk about the types because some didn't know the differences
   Find good sources to back up my knowlege

Sample Informative Preparation Outline

Don't Let Time Manage You

Topic: Time Management
Organization: Topical
Specific Purpose: To inform my audience about some practical time management tips.

I. **INTRODUCTION**

   A. **Attention Getter:**   Dr. Seuss once wisely remarked, "How did it get so late so soon? It's night before it's afternoon. December is here before it's June. My goodness how the time has flewn. How did it get so late so soon?" (Brainy-Quote, n.d.).

   B. **Relevance:**   Time management is something that we all have to learn as college students, whether we like it or not.

   C. **Credibility Statement:**   Just like you, I too have mountains of homework and classes to attend, and I have the same 24-hour day that you do! While I can't say that I have mastered the art of time management completely, I have learned some things from my own experience as well as researched some strategies to help us get the most out of our day.

   D. **Central Idea:**   In order to get the most out of our day, it is important to understand how we can manage our time.

   E. **Initial Preview:**   We will learn how to manage our time by identifying time wasters, setting goals, and keeping the right perspective.

Transition to 1st main point: First, let's talk about <u>identifying time wasters</u>.

II. **BODY**

   A. Before we can improve our time management skills, we have to understand where our time is going.

   1. In the article "How to Manage Time With 10 Tips That Work" from *Entrepreneur*.com, the first step identified is to write down what activities you do during a week's time (Mathews, Debolt, & Percival, 2011).

   2. One of the most common time wasters is the internet. *Business News Daily* reported in 2013 that the average internet user spends 23 hours a week online, 14% of the total hours in a week (Mielach, 2013).

   3. A really great way to see where your time online goes is to use a tracking application such as RescueTime. According to a review by *PC World* (and my own personal experience), this application can be downloaded through Google Chrome and tracks the amount of time you spend on each site (Zukerman, 2013). If you ever needed to be more convinced of the need to kick your Facebook habit, this app will do it for you.

Transition to 2nd main point: Now that we've talked about <u>identifying time wasters</u>, let's see how <u>setting goals</u> can help.

   B. Successful time management depends on setting reachable goals.

   1. Be sure that when you set goals for what you want to accomplish, your goals are realistic. Dr. Traci Stein, PhD, writes, "[O]ne of the simplest but most effective strategies is to break large, daunting goals into discreet, manageable tasks. Completing each task gives us evidence of success, and decreases the anxiety related to the larger aim" (Stein, 2013).

   2. If you are overwhelmed by the size of your goals, remember that your goals need to be S.M.A.R.T.—specific, measurable, attainable, relevant, and time-bound. An article called "Personal Goal Setting" from MindTools.com points out that using these criteria to set goals will help them be more powerful in the long run (Personal Goal Setting, n.d.).

3. For example, the next time that you sit down to knock out your homework, rather than saying, "I want to get everything done!" try using the SMART goal strategy. Instead, say that you will study for an hour for that exam that is coming up and spend at least 30 minutes writing the first draft of your paper that is due next week. These goals are specific, measurable, attainable, relevant, and time-bound.

Transition to 3rd main point: Now that we've discussed <u>identifying time wasters</u> and <u>setting reachable goals</u>, let's discuss <u>keeping the right perspective</u>.

C.   Time management will be far more successful if we keep the right perspective through it all.

1. Most of the time, we approach time management as a tool to make us happier. After all, if I manage my time better, then I'll have more time to spend doing things that make me happy. However, according to an article on productivity from the Huffington Post, research shows that "success follows happiness not the other way around" (Kuhel, 2015).

2. So what can we do to be happier? This same article recommends exercising, meditating, writing down positive experiences, and expressing praise and gratitude toward others, among other things, as ways to develop a happier, more optimistic outlook on life (Kuhel, 2015).

III. CONCLUSION

A.   **Transition to Conclusion:**   In conclusion,

B.   **Restate Central Idea:**   Time management is an important skill to master.

C.   **Final Summary:**   Today, we discussed how identifying time wasters, setting goals, and keeping the right perspective can help us on our journey to keeping control over our time.

D.   **Memorable Closing:**   I don't know about Dr. Seuss, but the rest of us only have 24 hours in a day, so it's important to make the most of the time you have. Manage your time instead of letting time manage you.

References

BrainyQuote. (n.d.). Dr. Suess quotes. Retrieved from http://www.brainyquote.com/quotes/quotes/d/drseuss109087.html

Kuhel, B. (2015). To increase productivity: Work less, get happy. *Huffington Post*. Retrieved from http://www.huffingtonpost.com/beth-kuhel/to-increase-productivity-_b_6639482. html

Mathews, J., Debolt, D., & Percival, D. (2011). How to manage time with 10 tips that work. *Entrepreneur*. Retrieved from http://www.entrepreneur.com/article/219553

Mielach, D. (2013). Americans spent 23 hours per week online, texting. *Business Week Daily*. Retrieved from http://www.businessnewsdaily.com/4718-weekly-online-social-media-time.html

Personal goal setting. (n.d.). *Mind tools*. Retrieved from http://www.mindtools.com/page6.html

Stein, T. (2013). Kicking the procrastination "habit." *Psychology Today*. Retrieved from https://www.psychologytoday.com/blog/the-integrationist/201303/kicking-the-procrastination-habit

Zukerman, E. (2013). Review: RescueTime helps you figure out where your week went. *PC World*. Retrieved from http://www.pcworld.com/article/2066770/review-rescuetime-helps-you-figure-out-where-your-week-went.html

Informative Presentation Speaking Notes

Don't Let Time Manage You

INTRO

- "How did it get so late so soon? It's night before it's afternoon. December is here before it's June. My goodness how the time has flewn. How did it get late so soon?" – Dr. Seuss
- We need time management in college.
- I have learned a lot about time management.
- In order to get the most out of our day, it's important to understand how we can manage our time.
- Today we will learn:
  1. Identifying time wasters
  2. Setting goals
  3. Keeping the right perspective

Point 1: Identifying time wasters

- Article: "How to Manage Time With 10 Tips That Work" from *Entrepreneur*.com, first step write down what you do.
- Article: Business News (Daily, 2013), average user online 23 hours per week, 14% of the week.
- Use the app RescueTime to track online activities. Article: *PC World*.

Point 2: Setting goals

- Article: Dr. Traci Stein, break tasks down into smaller tasks.
- Article: "Personal Goal Setting" from MindTools, use SMART goals.
- Personal example, try setting specific, measureable, attainable, relevant, and time-bound goals.

Point 3: Keeping the right perspective

- Article: Huffington Post, success follows happiness, not the other way around.
- Same article recommends exercising, expressing gratitude, writing down positive experiences, helping cultivate an optimistic attitude.

CONCLUSION

- Time management is an important skill to master.
- Review: identifying time wasters, setting goals, keeping the right perspective.
- Manage your time, don't let time manage you.

Sample Informative Preparation Outline

HEY! We're RHA

Topic: Residence Hall Association
Organization: Topically
Specific Purpose: To inform my audience about what the Residence Hall Association does at Texas State University.

I. INTRODUCTION

A. **Attention Getter:**   Residence Hall Association is part of the largest completely student-run organization in the world, the National Association of Collegiate and University Residence Halls.

B. **Relevance:**   RHA is the voice for students when it comes to everything from parking, dining halls, and housing rules to the costs of those things and more.

C. **Credibility Statement:**   This year I was president of Laurel/Retama Hall council for RHA, and next year I will be the national communications coordinator for the RHA Executive Board for Texas State University.

D. **Central Idea:**   The Residence Hall Association is an important campus group that does good work.

E. **Initial Preview:**   By the end of this speech, I will have informed you about what RHA is, how they're involved in student affairs, and the events that they host for students.

Transition to 1ˢᵗ main point: First, let's find out what the Residence Hall Association is at Texas State University.

II. BODY

A.   Point #1: RHA is an organization stationed in the Department of Housing based around student representation and residence hall improvement.

1. RHA has student councils to represent each residence hall on campus, an executive board that oversees the whole campus, and regional and national affiliations to connect students and share ideas for improving residence hall experiences.

2. "RHA offers programming, leadership opportunities, and support for all students who live on campus. Additionally, RHA works closely with the Residence Life staff, and through legislation, is charged with addressing the concerns of all residents and how to make their life on campus change for the better" (Overview, 2013).

3. Like I said in the introduction, everybody who lives in a residence hall is a member and can get involved in the university through RHA.

Transition to 2ⁿᵈ main point: Now that we understand what RHA is, let's examine further in detail what RHA does on campus.

B.   Point #2: RHA represents student interests all over campus.

1. RHA also sends student representatives to sit in on committees to do with everything on campus from changes at the dining halls to construction on campus, and even transportation and parking services.

2. "Texas State University has announced the most diverse student body in the school's history, part of a record-setting enrollment of 35,568 for the 2013 fall semester" (Blaschke, 2013).

3. The RHA Organization is involved in every major change that occurs on campus and affects you.

Transition to 3rd main point: Now that we have seen what RHA is and what it does, let's take a closer look at some RHA events.

C.   Point #3: The Residence Hall Association throws multiple events on campus each semester that are free and open to all students on campus.

1.   This year RHA hosted a Zombie Prom event, a silent auction/talent show charity benefit for Holiday Hope, and an Art Show Gala focused around the University 2013–2014 "Minds Matter" theme.

2.   "Programming is essential to every Residence Hall Association. It is often the best way to get students involved with the RHA and is also a great way to expand leadership opportunities within your organization" (NACURH, 2005).

3.   These are free events students can go to and have fun! There's always free food and most of the time prizes, awards, and fun games to play!

Transition to Conclusion: There are many things RHA is involved in that students don't seem to know about. In conclusion,

III. CONCLUSION

A.   **Restate Central Idea:**   Residence Hall Association is a huge organization on campus and is the main form of student representation at Texas State University.

B.   **Final Summary:**   RHA is a student organization run through the Department of Housing, represents the on-campus student body at all university departmental meetings, and throws free events for students on campus.

C.   **Memorable Closing:**   I'm glad I could inform members of the largest student organization about what they're a part of.

References

Blaschke, J. (2013). Texas State sets enrollment record for 16th consecutive year. Texas State University. Retrieved from http://www.txstate.edu/news/news_releases/news_archive/2013/September2013/Enrollment091613.html

Overview. (2013). Texas State University. Retrieved from http://rha.reslife.txstate.edu/about/overview.html

NACURH (2005). Guide to Beginning an RHA. Retrieved from http://www.nacurh.org/docs/buildRHA.pdf

SOURCE: Kuykendall, Joseph. Used with permission.

Informative Presentation Speaking Notes

Hey! We're RHA

INTRO

- RHA is part of largest student-run organization in the world.
- RHA is relevant because it is here on campus.
- Talk about personal experience being involved in RHA.
- The Residence Hall Association is an important campus group that does good work.
- Preview:

  1. What RHA is
  2. How they are involved in student affairs
  3. What events they host for students

Point 1: What RHA is

- Student councils represent each res hall, executive board, regional/national affiliations.
- Article: Texas State University, "RHA offers programming, leadership opportunities, and support for all students who live on campus. Additionally, RHA works closely with the Residence Life staff, and through legislation, is charged with addressing the concerns of all residents and how to make their life on campus change for the better."
- Anyone can get involved if they live in a res hall.

Point 2: What RHA does

- Student representatives
- Article: News release from Texas State University, TXST has most diverse student body in the history of the school.
- RHA is involved in every major change that takes place on campus.

Point 3: RHA events

- Zombie Prom, silent auction/talent show charity, Art Show Gala, etc.
- Article: National Association of Collegiate and University Residence Halls, programming is very important for getting students involved with RHA.
- The events are free, have free food, sometimes have prizes and awards.

CONCLUSION

- RHA is a huge organization on campus, main form of student representation at Texas State.
- Review:

  1. What RHA is
  2. What RHA does
  3. RHA events

- I'm glad to inform you about this organization that you all can be a part of.

SOURCE: Kuykendall, Joseph. Used with permission.

Sample Informative Preparation Outline

"Joan Jett: Lover of Rock N' Roll"

Topic: Joan Jett
Organization: Chronological
Specific Purpose: To inform my audience about the successes of Joan Jett's rock career.

I. INTRODUCTION

A. **Attention Getter:**   Lover of rock n' roll, feminist icon, and black leather. What do these have in common? Joan Jett, of course.

B. **Relevance:**   Joan Jett has produced many songs, including "I Love Rock N' Roll" and "Bad Reputation." Joan Jett also performed in sold-out shows with Aerosmith and Queen.

C. **Credibility Statement:**   I have been a huge fan of Joan Jett since I was a little girl when my dad played "I Love Rock N' Roll" for me. I also own several of her albums such as *Up Your Ally* and *Bad Reputation.*

D. **Central Idea:**   Joan Jett started her music career as an eager 14-year-old and became the Queen of Rock N' Roll.

E. **Initial Preview:**   Throughout this speech you will learn about how Joan Jett got started, her most famous years, and her successes today.

Transition to 1ˢᵗ main point: First, let's talk about how Joan Jett got started.

II. BODY

A. Point #1: Joan Jett was born Joan Larkin in Philadelphia and moved with her family to Southern California when she decided she wanted to pursue a career in music.

1. According to Rolling Stone (2015), Joan Jett received her first guitar at the age of 14 and was continuously inspired to become a great guitarist while listening to some of her favorite artists like T. Rex, Slade, David Bowie, and Suzi Quatro.

2. At the age of 15, Joan Jett was approached by producer Kim Fowley and was asked to join his band, The Runaways. This led to Joan becoming a founding member.

3. Also according to Rolling Stone (2015), Joan Jett helped produce great songs with The Runaways like "Cherry Bomb," and the band toured around the world opening for famous bands like The Ramones, Cheap Trick, and Van Halen. The Runaways were very popular in Europe, Australia, Asia, and Canada, but they could not gain the same level of success in the U.S.

Transition to 2ⁿᵈ main point: Now that we've talked about how Joan Jett got started with music, let's talk about her most famous years.

B. Point #2: Because The Runaways were unsuccessful in the U.S., they disbanded. This allowed Joan Jett to move on to bigger and better things.

1. According to Erlewine (2014), Joan Jett started her solo career and produced her first record, "Bad Reputation." The song was a hit in the U.S. and eventually became the well-known pop-punk anthem that you hear in movies today. It wasn't long after that Joan assembled The Blackhearts. It was for this band that Joan produced the iconic song "I Love Rock N' Roll," which was number 1 on the Billboard chart for 7 weeks.

2. Joan Jett and The Blackhearts became one of the first bands to perform multiple sold-out shows on Broadway at the Lunt-Fontanne Theatre. It was after this that she released *Up Your Ally,* which became multi-platinum. Later, according

to Erlewine (2014), Joan Jett was dubbed the titles "Godmother of Punk" and the "Original Riot Grrrl."

Transition to 3ʳᵈ main point: Now that we've discussed how Joan Jett got started and her successes, let's discuss what Joan Jett's doing today.

    C. Point #3: Despite not producing any more new music, Joan Jett is still active in the music scene today by releasing revamped songs and touring around the world.

      1. According to IMDB (2015), Joan Jett and The Blackhearts were nominated for the Rock and Roll Hall of Fame in 2012, and in 2013 she released the album *Unvarnished*, which contains many of her most popular songs.

      2. In 2010, Joan Jett co-produced the movie *The Runaways*, which starred Kristen Stewart as Joan Jett and Dakota Fanning, who played her band mate Cherie Currie. This movie was about a 1970s all-girl rock band. The movie grossed about $5 million and received favorable reviews from critics.

      3. Recently, Hot Topic released a clothing line based on Joan Jett's style, and she played guitar on the Foo Fighter's 2014 *Sonic Highways* album. Joan Jett is still touring around the world today and can be seen in Austin on tour with The Who in April.

III. CONCLUSION

Transition to Conclusion: In conclusion,

    D. Restate Central Idea: Since she was 14 Joan Jett worked hard to become the successful woman she is today.

    E. Final Summary: Joan Jett started her career with The Runaways, which brought her to her huge successes like The Blackhearts, and is currently still working with the music industry today.

    F. Memorable Closing: As Joan Jett once said, "There's nothing better than seeing a three-chord straight-up rock 'n' roll band in your face with sweaty music and 3-minute good songs."

References

Rolling Stone. (2015). *Joan Jett*. Retrieved from http://www.rollingstone.com/music/artists/joan-jett/biography

IMDB. (2015). *Joan Jett: Biography*. Retrieved from http://www.imdb.com/name/nm0005053/bio?ref_=nm_ov_bio_sm

Erlewine, S. T. (2014). About Joan Jett. *MTV Artists*. Retrieved from http://www.mtv.com/artists/joan-jett/biography/i

Informative Presentation Speaking Notes

"Joan Jett: Lover of Rock N' Roll"

INTRO

- Lover of rock n' roll, feminist icon, and black leather. What do these have in common? Joan Jett of course.
- Joan Jett has performed in sold out concerts with Queen and Aerosmith.
- I have been a huge fan since I was a little girl.
- Joan Jett started her music career as an eager 14-year-old and became the Queen of Rock N' Roll.
- Today we will lea rn:

  1. Start of her career
  2. Famous years
  3. Her successes today

Point 1: How Joan Jett's Career started

- Article: Rolling Stone said that Joan Jett was born as Joan Larkin and got her first guitar at the age of 14.
- David Bowie, Slade, and T. Rex continuously inspired Joan Jett.
- Joan Jet started with The Runaways and opened with famous bands like The Ramones, Cheap Trick, and Van Halen.

Point 2: Famous years

- Article: Erlewine reported that Joan Jett started her solo career with the album *Bad Reputation,* and the title song became a well known pop-legend song in most movies.
- It wasn't long until she started Joan Jett and The Blackhearts and produced the iconic song "I Love Rock N' Roll."
- Joan Jett became well known in the feminist Punk Rock movement Riot Grrrl and was known as the original "Riot Grrrl" and "Godmother of Punk."

Point 3: Successes today

- According to IMDB Joan Jett and the Blackhearts were nominated for the Rock and Roll Hall of fame in 2012.
- Joan Jett co-produced the movie *The Runaways,* which starred Kristen Stewart as Joan Jett and Dakota Fanning as her childhood friend and lead singer of The Runaways, Cherrie Currie.
- Hot Topic is currently selling a clothing line based on Joan Jett's rock style. And she is currently touring with The Who this year.

CONCLUSION

- Joan Jett worked hard to become the successful woman she is today.
- Review: Start of her career, famous years, and her successes today.
- "There's nothing better than seeing a three-chord straight-up rock 'n' roll band in your face with sweaty music and 3-minute good songs." – Joan Jett.

Sample Informative Preparation Outline

The Statues in the Quad

Topic: The Three Statues Throughout the Texas State Quad
Organization: Spatial
Specific Purpose: I would like my audience to understand the history of the three statues in our university's quad.

I. **INTRODUCTION**
   A. **Attention Getter:**   Naked men fighting on stallions, a larger-than-life bobcat, and a former president of the United States. What do they all have in common? They are immortalized as statues in our university's quad.
   B. **Relevance:**   We all walk past these pieces of art on a daily basis, but not many people know the history behind them. It is important that we understand our past so we can pass that knowledge to future generations of students.
   C. **Credibility Statement:**   As a member of the Texas State Student Foundation, I give tours to distinguished alumni and special guests visiting our campus. Part of that responsibility is knowing the history of our campus, including the public art such as these statues.
   D. **Central Idea:**   The three statues in the quad are more than pieces of art. They are representative of Texas State's history.
   E. **Initial Preview:**   Today we will go on a walk through the quad and learn about The Fighting Stallions, The Bobcat Statue, and the LBJ Statue.

Transition: Let's begin our journey between Derrick Hall and Evans Liberal Arts, the location of the Fighting Stallions statue.

II. **BODY**
   A.   The Fighting Stallion Statue anchors one end of our quad and has been subject to controversy and traditions since its installation.
      1. According to the Texas State History and Traditions Web page, the stallions stand 17 feet tall and also serve as the university's designated free speech area (Fighting stallions, 2010). That is why any time you see preachers, protestors, or other people promoting their ideas, it always takes place by the statue.
      2. The statue was originally very controversial. A women sculptor created it, and at the time many decades ago it was frowned upon for a woman artist to sculpt naked men such as those riding the stallions. When the statue was given to the university as a gift, it was placed far away from the center of campus, which at the time was Old Main. Ironically, the attempt to place the statue out of the way backfired as the campus expanded over the years.
      3. In addition to controversy, the Fighting Stallions are also part of a popular unofficial tradition. Students believe that rubbing the stallions' testicles prior to taking an exam will bring them good luck and good grades.

Transition: Now let us continue our journey to the middle of the quad where we find the Bobcat Statue.

   B.   The Bobcat Statue was installed in 2008 and is the newest public art addition to the Texas State Quad.
      1. The statue was commissioned by the Associated Student Government, and the student body voted to allocate a portion of existing student fees to pay for its creation.
      2. However, according to a University Star article from April 2009, shortly after the statue was dedicated, someone wrote on its base, "Give us lower tuition, not statues" (McSpadden, 2009). This sums up an ongoing debate about how the

university uses its funds, specifically in the midst of an emphasis in upgrading our athletic program during a financial recession.

3. You may have also noticed a small chain a foot off of the ground surrounding the statue. This seemingly decorative divider was actually installed shortly after the statue's installation. A visually impaired student injured himself by running into the statue, which protrudes off the base upon which it sits. As a safety precaution the chain was added so the visually impaired who use a white cane to walk around campus would be alerted of the statue.

Transition: Now that we've talked about the Bobcat Statue, let's head in the direction of Old Main and stop at the LBJ Statue along the way.

C. President Lyndon Baines Johnson is Texas State's most influential and famous alum; thus, it is fitting that the university has commemorated him with a statue.

1. The statue depicts LBJ as a student, and he is holding a book in one hand and extending his hand outward as if he is leading his fellow students to class.
2. The statue originally did not stand upon a marble base, giving the appearance that LBJ was just another student in the crowded quad.
3. According to a 2008 article in the San Marcos Mercury, two students vandalized the statue by covering it with napalm and setting it ablaze (Rollins, 2008).
4. Similar to the vandalism that occurred to the Bobcat Statue, this illegal act is symbolic of the conflicting feelings students and alumni have toward LBJ and his presidency. While the university chooses to celebrate LBJ's significant domestic accomplishments, others do not believe the university should celebrate the president who prolonged the Vietnam War.

III. CONCLUSION

A. **Transition:** In conclusion,

B. **Restate Central Idea:** These statues are more than just art—they are symbols of our university's history.

C. **Final Summary:** We learned about the controversy of The Fighting Stallions, the more recent installation of the Bobcat Statue, and the importance of the LBJ Statue.

D. **Memorable Closing:** We have all walked by these statues dozens if not hundreds of times. Next time you walk through the quad, which could be as soon as after this class is over, take the time to admire and think about these statues and the role they play in Texas State's history.

References

Fighting stallions. (2010). Retrieved from http://www.txstate.edu/about/history-traditions/fighting-stallions.html

McSpadden, G. (2009, April 1). Students can implement change in government. *The University Star.* Retrieved from http://star.txstate.edu/content/students-can-implement-change-government

Rollins, B. (2008, February 17). Nearing LBJ's centennial, Texas State looks to its most famous alumnus to help shape identity. *San Marcos Mercury.* Retrieved from http://smmercury. com/2008/02/17/nearing-lbj's-centennial-texas-state-looks-to-its-most-famous-alumnus-to-help-shape-identity/

Informative Presentation Speaking Notes

The Statues in the Quad

INTRO

- Naked men fighting on stallions, a larger-than-life bobcat, and a former president of the United States ....
- We are all students at Texas State.
- I am a member of the Texas State Student Foundation, tour guide, etc.
- The three statues in the quad are more than pieces of art. They are representative of Texas State's history.
- Today we will walk through the quad and learn about
  1. The Fighting Stallions
  2. The Bobcat Statue
  3. The LBJ Statue

Point 1: The Fighting Stallions

- <u>Article:</u> from the Texas State History and Traditions Web site, stallions are 17 feet high, serve as free speech area.
- Originally controversial because it was created by a woman sculptor. It was considered inappropriate for a woman to sculpt naked men. As a result it was placed far away from the center of campus (Old Main).
- Popular, unofficial tradition: rubbing stallions' testicles brings good luck for exams.

Point 2: The Bobcat Statue

- Commissioned by student government, paid for by existing student fees.
- <u>Article:</u> *University Star,* April 2009 (McSpadden, 2009), someone wrote "Give us lower tuition, not statues" on the base of the statue. Thus, this is still controversial.
- Small chain around the statue to help visually impaired students, due to previous injury.

Point 3: The LBJ Statue

- Depicts LBJ holding book, extending hand to lead students to class.
- Originally wasn't on a marble base, made LBJ look like he was a student in the crowd.
- <u>Article:</u> San Marcos Mercury, 2008, two students vandalized the statue by covering it in napalm and setting it on fire.
- Like Bobcat Statue vandalism, this represents feelings students have about LBJ and his involvement in the Vietnam War. Students have mixed feelings. The university still decides to celebrate LBJ's successes.

CONCLUSION

- These statues are more than art—they are symbols of the university's history.
- Review: the Fighting Stallions, Bobcat Statue, and LBJ Statue.
- Next time you walk through the quad, think about the role these statues play in Texas State's history.

Study Guide for Communicating in the Informative Speaking Context Module

Chapter 11 Developing Your Presentation

1. Be able to **identify** the eight steps involved in the audience-centered model of the public speaking process: selecting and narrowing a topic, identifying purpose, developing a central idea, generating main ideas, gathering supporting material, organizing your speech, rehearsing your speech, and delivering your speech.

2. Be able to **explain** how each of the following methods help speakers manage their anxiety: knowing how to develop a presentation, being prepared, focusing on your audience, focusing on your message, giving yourself a mental pep talk, using deep-breathing techniques, seeking opportunities to speak, and seeking professional help.

3. Be able to **differentiate** the general purpose from the specific purpose statement of a speech.

4. Be able to **differentiate** the specific purpose statement from the central idea of a speech.

5. Be able to **list** and **identify** the types of supporting material: illustrations, descriptions and explanations, definitions, analogies, statistics, and opinions.

6. Be able to **identify** when to use the 5 Principles of Communication as you're developing your presentation.

Chapter 12 Organizing and Outlining Your Presentation

1. Be able to **identify** three methods of organizing your main ideas in informative speaking: chronological, topical, and spatial.

2. Be able to **identify** four methods of organizing your supporting material: chronologically, recency, primacy, and complexity.

3. Be able to **identify** initial previews, transitions, and final summaries.

4. Be able to **recall** six functions of an introduction: gaining attention, introducing topic, creating a reason to listen, establishing credibility, stating central idea, and previewing main ideas.

5. Be able to **recall** three functions of a conclusion in informative speaking: summarizing the presentation, reemphasizing the central idea, and providing closure.

6. Be able to **differentiate** a preparation outline and speaking notes.

7. Be able to **recall** suggestions for developing speaking notes.

Chapter 14 Speaking to Inform

1. Be able to **differentiate** informative from persuasive speaking.

2. Be able to **identify** and **differentiate** the types of informative presentations: presentations about objects, presentations about procedures, presentations about people, presentations about events, and presentations about ideas.

3. Be able to **identify** and **recall** strategies for making your informative presentation clear, including using simple ideas rather than complex ones, pacing your information flow, and relating new information to old information.

4. Be able to **identify** and **recall** strategies for making your informative presentation interesting to your audience including presenting information that relates to your

listeners' interests, using attention-catching supporting material, establishing a motive for your audience to listen to you, using word pictures, creating interesting presentation aids, and using humor.

5. Be able to **identify** strategies for making your presentation memorable, including building in redundancy and reinforcing key ideas verbally and nonverbally.

6. Be able to **identify** the 5 Principles of Communication when speaking to inform.

Sample Exam Questions
Module: Communicating in the Informative Speaking Context

Chapter 11   Developing Your Presentation

1. Rodney notices that the audience is racially and ethnically diverse. He is careful not to make generalizations that might offend anyone during his speech. What type of speaker is Rodney?
   A. Audience-centered
   B. Self-centered
   C. Other-centered
   D. People-centered

2. Jill gives a speech on the fourth of July about America's independence. Jill's speech topic reveals a careful analysis of:
   A. Her interests
   B. The occasion
   C. Her experiences
   D. The audience

3. After gaining the attention of the audience, Tom states, "At the end of my speech, the audience will be able to explain the causes and most successful treatments for anorexia and bulimia." This statement is which of the following?
   A. General purpose statement
   B. Claim of policy
   C. Specific purpose statement
   D. Claim of value

4. Speakers should include a statement in their introduction that includes a discussion of their three main points in order to provide structure and organization to their informative presentations. This statement is considered a(n):
   A. General purpose
   B. Central idea
   C. Initial preview
   D. Specific purpose

5. Terri works for a news magazine and is giving a presentation to a group of graduating college students. A college graduate herself, she is relating her experiences in the workplace and needs to find a way to connect with her audience. Finally, she decides to relate the experience of cramming for final exams to reaching a publishing deadline. Terri is using supporting material that focuses on linking new information to a familiar concept. This type of supporting material is called:
   A. Analogy
   B. Definition
   C. Description
   D. Anecdote

Chapter 12   Organizing and Outlining Your Presentation

1.   The first main point of Elsa's speech focuses on Elton John's childhood. Her second main point focuses on his rise to fame, and her third main point emphasizes his current projects. What type of organizational pattern is Elsa using?

   A.   Topical
   B.   Spatial
   C.   Logical
   D.   Chronological

2.   Bradley states his strongest piece of evidence first. He states his weakest piece of evidence last. What method is Bradley using to organize his supporting material?

   A.   Specificity
   B.   Recency
   C.   Primacy
   D.   Complexity

3.   To adapt a logically organized message to an audience, a speaker must provide organizational cues for the audience. The speaker can do this by adding previews, verbal and nonverbal transitions, and summaries that allow the audience to follow from one idea to the other throughout the speech. These organizational cues are known as:

   A.   Main ideas
   B.   Closure
   C.   Outline
   D.   Signposts

4.   Mark is preparing a speech that he will present to his business class. He is unsure as to whether his material is comprehensive and well organized. In preparing an outline, he uses a format that allows him to examine the speech for completeness, unity, coherence, and overall effectiveness. This outline also serves as his rehearsal outline. This format is known as:

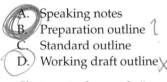

   A.   Speaking notes
   B.   Preparation outline
   C.   Standard outline
   D.   Working draft outline

5.   Clint wrote the words "pause" and "louder" in certain points on his speaking notes. The words he wrote are examples of:

   A.   Delivery cues
   B.   Preparation outlines
   C.   Delivery outlines
   D.   Signposts

Chapter 14   Speaking to Inform

1.   Nicholas wants to enhance the audience's knowledge and understanding of baseball. The general purpose of his speech will be to:

   A.   Entertain
   B.   Inform
   C.   Persuade
   D.   Teach

2.   Marianna wants to give a speech on how to make chocolate chip cookies from her aunt's recipe. Her informative speech will be about:

   A.   Objects
   B.   Procedures
   C.   People
   D.   Ideas

3. Which of the following strategies will enhance the clarity of an informative message?
   A. Use complex ideas
   B. Present information too quickly
   C. Show how new information relates to old information
   D. Present information too slowly

4. Masayuki gave a speech on ways the high-context values are reflected in the Japanese culture. His three main points were the language, the gift-giving customs, and the visual arts. Which pattern did he use to organize his speech?
   A. Topical
   B. Chronological
   C. Logical
   D. Spatial

5. Angela must present a speech advocating the name change at Texas State. In making the presentation memorable, she advances her ideas in the introduction, she expands on her ideas in the body, and she restates her ideas in the conclusion. In short, she repeats key ideas and major points throughout the speech. Which of the following strategies is she using?
   A. Establishing a motive for the audience to listen
   B. Building in redundancy
   C. Reinforcing key ideas verbally
   D. Reinforcing key ideas nonverbally

Answer Key

CHAPTER 11

1. A
2. B
3. C
4. C
5. A

CHAPTER 12

1. D
2. C
3. D
4. B
5. A

CHAPTER 14

1. B
2. B
3. C
4. A
5. B

MODULE 4
COMMUNICATING IN SMALL GROUP AND TEAM CONTEXTS

After completing this module (Chapters 9, 10, 13, and 15), you will be able to:

PRINCIPLE 1
Be aware of your communication with yourself and others.

- Recall elements of a small group and be able to distinguish a small group from a "gathering of people."
- Recall advantages and disadvantages of working in small groups.
- Distinguish between groups and teams.
- Differentiate and identify communication behaviors that reflect roles, rules, norms, status, power, and cohesiveness.
- Identify the functional problem-solving communication behaviors that typify John Dewey's Reflective Thinking Process.
- Define and distinguish task, social, and individual roles in groups.
- Recall and identify the symptoms of groupthink.
- Understand the ethical implications involved in group problem solving.

PRINCIPLE 2
Efficiently use and interpret verbal messages.

- Identify the process by which norms evolve and influence the group process through verbal messages.
- Identify the essential social roles of the harmonizer, encourager, tension reliever, and gatekeeper, using appropriate verbal messages.
- Use appropriate verbal messages to reach a decision by consensus.
- Send supportive verbal messages to group members about their ideas.
- Recognize moments when primary or secondary tension exists in a group, and provide release of that tension using appropriate verbal messages.
- Recognize moments during a discussion when there is uneven verbal interaction between group members, and serve as a catalyst to make the discussion more balanced.

PRINCIPLE 3
Effectively use and interpret nonverbal messages.

- Identify the process by which norms evolve and influence the group process through nonverbal messages.
- Recall and identify the role of nonverbal communication in harmonizing, encouraging, tension releasing, and gatekeeping group behaviors.
- Avoid negative or distracting nonverbal behavior during discussion.
- Send supportive nonverbal messages to group members about their ideas to establish and maintain a positive group climate.

PRINCIPLE 4
Listen and respond thoughtfully to others.

- Listen and put different ideas together during a group discussion so as to synthesize the ideas.
- Summarize ideas that are generated in a group discussion.
- Listen and ask follow-up questions in a discussion to foster elaboration on ideas.
- Give feedback during a discussion that allows a group to understand advantages to a possible solution to a problem.
- Critically evaluate the speaker's emotional appeal.

PRINCIPLE 5
Appropriately adapt messages to others.

- Identify and appropriately recommend the appropriate functional problem-solving behaviors for each stage of the group problem-solving process: identify and define problem, analyze problem, generate creative solutions, select best solution, and take action.
- Adapt messages to appropriately encourage less active group members to give input during discussions.
- Adapt messages to appropriately recognize moments when primary or secondary tension exists in a group and provide release of that tension.
- Recognize moments during a discussion when there is uneven interaction between group members and serve as a catalyst to make the discussion more balanced.
- Understand and apply one theory of persuasion (social judgment, dissonance, needs) to alter attitudes and behaviors of audience members.

Chapter 9
Lecture Notes

Chapter 10
Lecture Notes

Chapter 13
Lecture Notes

Chapter 15
Lecture Notes

Small Group Communication Module: Coloring Activity

Directions

Teams will be divided into groups of four. Each group will be given four colors. The goal for each group is to color in each page as quickly and neatly as possible. The group with the most pages completely colored and with the best quality wins. Your instructor will give you a color to match up with each number.

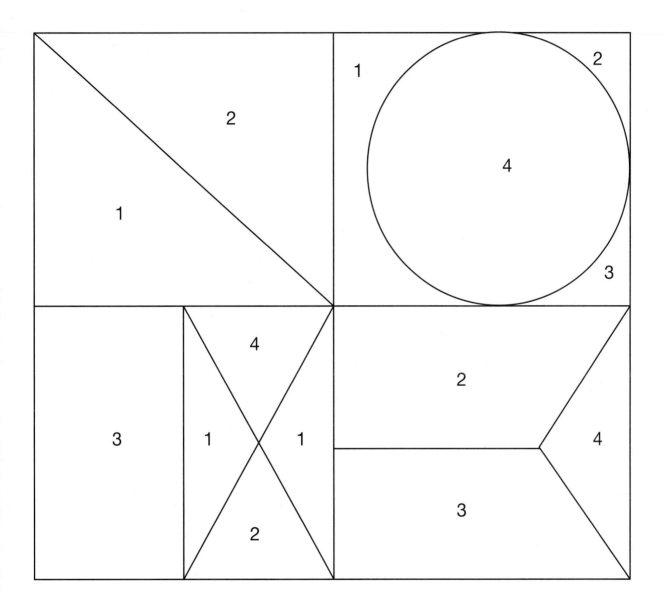

Coloring Activity/Group Problem-Solving Worksheet

1. Identify and define the problem.

    a. What is your problem?

    b. What is the felt difficulty or concern?

2. Analyze the problem.

    a. Where is the felt difficulty or concern located?

    b. What do you see as being the impelling and restraining forces?

3. Develop creative solutions through brainstorming or nominal group technique. Based on your very brief analysis, what are some creative solutions to the problem?

4. Evaluate the solution.

    a. What solution will best produce the desired results? How do you know this?

    b. What solution is most achievable? Note: Remember your time constraints.

5. Implement the plan.

    a. What specific tasks need to be completed?

    b. What is the most efficient way to accomplish these tasks?

Part II: Coloring Activity

Directions

Teams will be divided into groups of four. Each group will be given four colors. The goal for each group is to color in each page as quickly and neatly as possible. The group with the most pages completely colored and with the best quality wins.

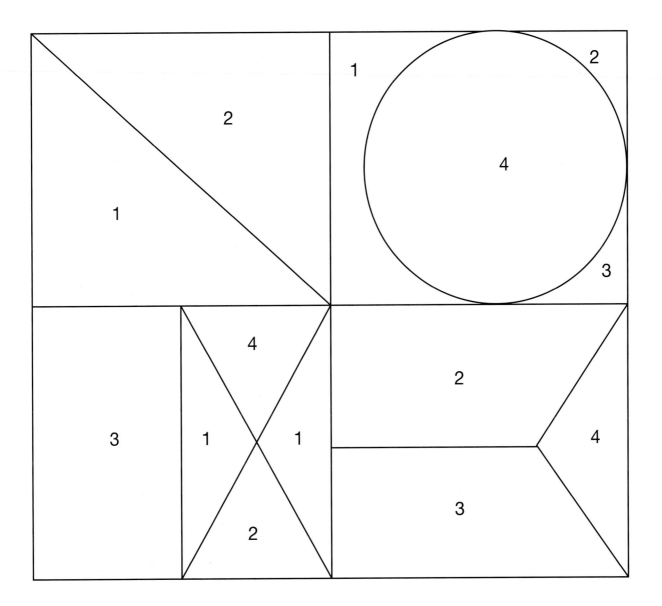

Small Group Communication Activity

Zombie Apocalypse Worksheet

The Earth has just been overrun by the living dead. Zombies are attacking every human within sight; however, they seem to be leaving all other animals alone. To make matters worse, the power has gone out, and you are stuck with the people whom you were with when the attack started. All your group has to survive is the skills that you have and several items that you have gathered. Unfortunately, your group has to leave their hideout in search of a place to hole up for the duration of the attack. Because of the size and weight of the items you have collected, you can only carry 10 items to your new safe house. Also, your group can only take one form of transportation and because there is no power you will need to siphon gas or you will run out. In addition, as your group is leaving you find several people who have fallen into a pit. Because time is short your group can only pick one person to save.

Priority = 1–10	Items (pick 10)
	Rope (200 ft; climbing style)
	Matches (pack of 500)
	Pile of lumber (2×4's, & 2×6's – 10 each)
	A large labrador retriever
21	Flashlights (3 LED motion rechargeable)
13	First aid kit (like you might have in a car)
	Pain medication (ibuprofen)
	Night vision goggles (1 replacement battery)
11	Ka-Bar knife
19	12-gauge shotgun (100 shells)
20	Pistol (150 rounds)
	Crossbow (10 bolts)
	Bow (15 arrows)
	Grenades (15)
	Flare gun (10 flares)
15	Body armor (4 sets)
	Camouflage
3	Scent neutralizer
	Map
2	Walkie-talkies (1 pair)
1	15 MREs (Meal, Ready to Eat)
23	Tool box (standard home/auto tools)
	A year's supply of Flintstone vitamins

Vehicle (pick 1)
'65 Chevy Impala
2005 Ford F250 diesel
2 horses with a wagon   20
'70 Volkswagen van

People in the Pit (pick 1)
Doctor (general practitioner)
Real estate lawyer
Civil engineer
Mechanical engineer
Comedian
Retired Navy Seal instructor   12
Demolitions expert
Psychiatrist
Fast food employee
A mountain man

Adapted from: Harris, B. (2011, November). Make critical thinking fun: The zombie apocalypse exercise. *Critical Thinkers*. Retrieved from http://critical-thinkers.com/2011/11/make-critical-thinking-fun-the-zombie-apocalypse-exercise

Small Group Communication Group Activity Worksheet

Complete the following questions as a group, using your textbook as a reference.

Can you define yourself as a small group? Why or why not?

Were you a team? Why or why not?

What type of group were you?

What norms did your group have?

Did your group have groupthink? Justify your answer.

Did you have a metadiscussion? Justify your answer.

Did you have a gatekeeper in your group? If so, who was it?

Did you reach a consensus?

Individual Assessment of a Group Project

Fill this out as an individual after completing a group project.

What role did you play as you completed the group project?

Who had power in your group, and what kind of power was it?

Name	Type of Power

Who did you perceive as the leader of your group?

What approach(es) did your leader take?

Rate your cohesiveness as a group.

❑ Not cohesive enough   ❑ Perfectly cohesive   ❑ Too cohesive

Justify your answer to how cohesive you were:

Group Creativity Activity:
It Can Do Something Else Corporation

Congratulations! You have been selected to be a part of the *It Can Do Something Else Corporation*! You and your group members will be given a mystery product that already serves a purpose in today's society. Your job as a group is to develop a new use or uses for this item and present a commercial to the CEO to convince him/her to use your advertisement to remarket this product and make the company millions! And remember the company's motto:

It might already be invented, but they'll still buy it!

Here are the rules:

1. You have 8 minutes to brainstorm and create a new purpose for the mystery product and a commercial to sell it.

2. You must change the name of the existing product and not mention its old name or current purpose in your commercial.

3. Your commercial cannot be longer than 2 minutes.

4. Every member of your group must speak at some time during the commercial.

5. Be creative and HAVE FUN!

ANY QUESTIONS?

IT CAN DO
**SOMETHING
ELSE**
CORPORATION

Hurricane Preparedness Case Study

Although you have idly watched local weather forecasters track Hurricane Bruce's destructive course throughout the Caribbean for several days, you have not really given any serious thought to the possibility that the Category 3 storm might directly affect your coastal city. But at about 7 o'clock this morning the storm suddenly veered northward, putting it on course for a direct hit. Now the National Hurricane Center in Miami has posted a hurricane warning for your community. Forecasters are predicting landfall in approximately 0 to 12 hours.

Having taken no advance precautions, you are stunned by the amount of work you now have to do to secure your three-bedroom suburban home, which is about a quarter mile from the beach. You have enough food in the house for 2 days. You also have a transistor radio with one weak battery and one candle. You have no other hurricane supplies, nor have you taken any hurricane precautions. Your task is to rank order the following items in terms of their importance for ensuring your survival and the safety of your property. Place number 1 by the first thing you should do, 2 by the second, and so on through number 13. Please work individually on this task.

Individual Ranking	Group Ranking
____ Fill your car with gas	____ Fill your car with gas
____ Trim your bushes and trees	____ Trim your bushes and trees
____ Fill your bathtub with water	____ Fill your bathtub with water
____ Construct hurricane shutters for your windows	____ Construct hurricane shutters for your windows
____ Buy enough food for a week	____ Buy enough food for a week
____ Buy batteries and candles	____ Buy batteries and candles
____ Bring in patio furniture from outside	____ Bring in patio furniture from outside
____ Buy dry ice	____ Buy dry ice
____ Invite friends over for a hurricane party	____ Invite friends over for a hurricane party
____ Drain your swimming pool	____ Drain your swimming pool
____ Listen to TV and radio before doing anything	____ Listen to TV and radio before doing anything
____ Make sure you have an evacuation plan	____ Make sure you have an evacuation plan
____ Stock up on charcoal and charcoal lighter for barbecue grill	____ Stock up on charcoal and charcoal lighter for barbecue grill

Adapted from: Beebe, S. A., & Masterson, J. T. (2009). *Communicating in Small Groups: Principles and Practices* (9th ed.). Boston, MA: Allyn and Bacon.

Group Problem Solving and Ethical Decision Making Assignment

Assignment Rationale

A survey of human resource managers revealed that oral communication (specifically, public speaking skills) remains the number one factor in helping graduating college students obtain employment. Research also shows that groups and teams come up with more creative solutions to problems than individuals working alone. These competencies will aid in more efficient and productive group and team communication, especially in workplace and public speaking contexts.

Assignment Expectations

The Group Problem Solving Assignment encourages and challenges you to understand and appreciate different points of view and work effectively with others to support a shared purpose or goal, and to understand the challenges of ethical decision making. You will work in teams of four to six people to analyze and solve a problem related to one of the five "We Are Bobcat Messages" that impacts the Texas State community. The "We Are Bobcat Messages" include: We Are Academically Successful, Caring, Diverse, Healthy, Responsible, and Proud.

Your group will use the problem-solving steps developed by Dewey (Chapter 10) to complete this assignment. As part of this problem-solving process, you will work with your group to discuss how your selected solution will ethically impact your audience. Finally, your group will give a **5–7 minute presentation** of the problem-solution process to your class using Monroe's Motivated Sequence.

Objectives

1. To conduct research in order to identify, define, and analyze a campus problem.

2. To work with group members to brainstorm creative solution ideas.

3. To work with group members to select the best solution based on criteria selected by the group and the resources available.

4. To provide a discussion of the consequences of their ethical decision making (who will be affected/how they will be affected if their solution is implemented).

5. To write a report identifying how the group implemented Dewey's various problem-solving stages.

6. To present their problem-solving process using Monroe's Motivated Sequence.

7. To learn that working in groups and teams requires *effective communication.*

8. To become aware that competence in communicating in groups and teams requires a combination of *knowledge, skills, and motivation.*

Directions

This is a four-part assignment that is worth **140 points**.

1. Topic Selection - not worth points, but must receive approval from instructor
2. Problem Solving Report - 40 points
3. Persuasive Presentation - 80 points
(this includes the preparation outline for 15 points, the actual delivery of the presentation for 60 points, and the speaking notes for 5 points)
4. Group Member Assessment - 20 points

Part 1: Students will select a campus-based problem from a list provided by their instructor. Working in groups of four to six, students will apply the stages of Dewey's problem-solving process to their specific problem. Groups will be asked to turn in a worksheet in which they identify the selected problem.

Part 2: Students will turn in a written report in which they document how they applied each of the stages of Dewey's problem-solving process to their specific problem. **The report is worth 40 points**. In this report, students must answer the following questions:

Identify and Define the Problem

- *What is the specific problem? Why is this a problem?*
- *What do we want more or less of?*
- *What terms need defining?*

Analyze the Problem

- *How long has this been a problem?*
- *How widespread is the problem?*
- *What are the causes of the problem?*
- *What are the effects of the problem?*
- *What has been done in the past?*
- *Develop specific and observable criteria or standards for an acceptable solution.*

Generate Creative Solution Ideas

- *List at least three ideas for solving the problem.*

Select the Best Solution

- *Does the solution meet the criteria?*
- *Does the solution solve the problem in both the short and long term?*
- *Do we have the resources to implement the solution?*
- *What consequences will implementing the solution have on the campus community?*
- *Who will be affected by the implementation of this solution?*
- *Why is the selected solution the best option for solving the problem?*

Part 3: In your groups, you will be required to present your problem and solution ideas using Monroe's Motivated Sequence. **This presentation is worth 80 points.** You will be required to turn in an initial outline of your presentation **(worth 15 points)** and a revised outline based on your instructor's feedback **(worth 5 points)**. The group presentation will be **worth 60 points.** In your presentation, each person on your team must present. Additionally, as a group you must include the following components in your presentation:

Attention

- *Gain audience's attention using statistics, quotes, etc. (See Chapter 12 for more ideas.)*
- *Attention getter should relate to your specific, campus-based problem.*

Need

- *Establish relevance with your audience—why should they care about this problem?*
- *How does this problem affect your classmates?*
- *Discuss the prevalence of the problem—provide evidence the problem exists.*

Satisfaction

- *Provide viable solution ideas.*

Visualization

- *Describe what will happen if your solution doesn't take place.*
- *Describe what will happen if your solution is implemented.*
- *Discuss which solution is the best choice and why.*

Action

- *Motivate your audience to take action.*
- *Provide them with specific instructions for helping to solve the problem.*

Part 4: You will be required to complete an assessment form for each member in your group. **This will be worth 20 points.**

Principles Targeted

1. **Be aware of your communication with yourself and others:** This assignment will challenge you to become more aware of how you communicate within group settings, for example, the roles you assume during group work.

2. **Effectively use and interpret verbal messages:** This assignment will require you to develop effective arguments through your use of reasoning and evidence during your oral presentation.

3. **Effectively use and interpret nonverbal messages:** This assignment will require you to use effective nonverbal delivery to persuade your audience.

4. **Listen and respond thoughtfully to others:** This assignment will challenge you to listen to your group members and to respond appropriately during the group problem-solving process. You will also need to listen thoughtfully as an audience member during the presentations.

5. **Appropriately adapt your messages to others:** This assignment will require you to adapt your messages to your audience while preparing for and delivering your oral presentation.

Part One: Topic Selection Worksheet

As a group, you will need to select one of the vital issues listed below and then narrow the topic to solve a problem that impacts the Texas State community:

We Are Bobcat Message:

- We Are Academically Successful

- We Are Caring

- We Are Diverse

- We Are Healthy

- We Are Responsible

- We Are Proud

Group Members' Names: Hunter, lily Kelsey.

Presentation Topic: accessibility to food

This directly impacts the members of my audience because: (How will we make it relevant?)

Brainstorm step one of Dewey's problem-solving process

- What is the specific problem? Why is it a problem?

- What do we want more or less of?

- What terms need defining? Define them here.

Possible sources include (Where can we find information about our problem and solution options?)

1. _____

2. _____

3. _____

Part Two: Dewey's Problem-Solving Process Report

Group Members' Names: _____

Instructions: As a group, you will answer each of the questions on this worksheet. Be sure to include full sentences in this report and cite at least three sources (at least one in steps 1, 2, and 5). This will be worth 40 points. You will be expected to use terminology from Chapters 9 and 10 to complete this assignment. You will also be expected to cite sources to back up each claim you make in this report.

Step One: Identify and Define the Problem

1. What is the specific problem that concerns us? Why is this a problem?

2. What do we want more or less of?

3. What terms, concepts, or ideas do we need to define in order to understand the problem? Define them here.

4. Who is harmed by the problem?

Step Two: Analyze the Problem

1. How long has the problem been in existence?

2. How widespread is the problem?

3. What are the causes of the problem?

4. What are the effects of the problem?

5. What methods already exist for managing the problem?

6. What are the limitations of existing methods?

7. What obstacles keep the group from achieving the goal? What resources exist to help the group achieve the goal? (Forcefield Analysis)

8. What are the criteria we have agreed upon?

Step Three: Generate Creative Solutions

1. What method did we use to create our solution ideas?

2. What rules did we adhere to during our brainstorming process?

3. What are three solution ideas we have generated?

Step Four: Select the Best Solution

1. How did we evaluate the solution ideas we came up with?

2. Which method did we use for selecting the best solution?

3. What communication strategies did we use during the evaluation process?

4. What is the final and best solution we decided on?

Step Five: Take Action

1. How do we know the solution will solve the problem?

2. What are the implications of selecting the proposed solution?

3. What are the implications of NOT selecting your other solution ideas?

Part Two: Dewey's Problem-Solving Process Report Assessment Form

Group Members' Names: _____

Report Information (15 points)

____ Problem is related to Texas State and "We Are Bobcats" message

____ Definition and analysis of problem was thorough

____ Evidence that problem exists included

____ At least 3 viable solutions identified

____ Evidence that solution will resolve or minimize the problem included

____ Consequences of implementing and NOT implementing solution are addressed

____ All required questions were answered thoroughly and thoughtfully

____ It is apparent that group members completed Dewey's problem-solving process

Group and Team Communication (5 points)

____ Minimum 4–5 terms included

____ Terms discussed in steps 2, 3, and 4

____ Terms are used appropriately

____ Terms are discussed thoroughly

Research Support (15 points)

____ Minimum 3 sources included

____ Sources cited in steps 1, 2, and 5

____ Included in-text citations in APA format

____ Included reference page in APA format

____ Claims were backed with evidence

Writing Style (5 points)

____ Answers to questions were in complete sentences

____ Responses followed proper grammar and spelling rules

____ Responses were professional in nature

Total Score: _____

Comments: _____

Persuasive Audience Adaptation Plan

Group Members' Names: _____

Presentation Topic: _____

Specific Presentation Goal: At the end of my presentation, my audience will believe/agree/consider:

This is what I know about my audience:

1. My audience's demographic profile: Sex: _____ Male _____ Female Average Age: _____
   Ethnicity: _____ Class Rank: _____ Fresh. _____ Soph. _____ Jr. _____ Sr. _____
   Group Memberships: _____
   _____

2. On a scale from 1 to 5 (1 = Low, 5 = High), how relevant and interesting is my two-part propositional statement to
   my audience? _____
   Write your two-part propositional statement here: _____
   _____
   _____
   _____

3. On a scale from 1 to 5 (1 = Little, 5 = A lot), my audience's level of knowledge about this problem is: _____
   Explain why you believe their knowledge of the problem would be at this level: _____
   _____
   _____
   _____

4. I would consider my audience's attitude towards my topic to be (check):
   _____ Receptive   _____ Neutral   _____ Unreceptive

   Explain why you believe that would be their attitude: _____
   _____
   _____
   _____

5. On a scale from 1 to 5 (1 = Little, 5 = A lot), my audience's perception of my credibility will be: _____
   _____

   Explain why you believe your audience will find you credible.

6. Based on the information, provide two specific examples of how you will adapt your presentation to this audience. _____
   _____
   _____
   _____

Part Three: Persuasive Presentation Preparation Outline Assessment Form (15 points)

Group Members' Names: _____

Topic: _____   **Total Score:** _____ /15

(+ = Excellent ✔ = Fair — = Poor)

Problem was selected from vital issues checklist

Problem is narrow

Problem is relevant to the audience

Used proper outline format – Roman numerals, letters, numbers (followed sample)

Specific purpose indicated

Problem/solution propositional statement included

3 well-developed main ideas with 1 source clearly cited in each

Problem(s) indicated and evidence included

Solution(s) indicated and evidence included

Final summary indicated – Conclusion and call to action

Transitions indicated throughout

Included bibliography with 3 different sources using APA format

Included completed Persuasive Audience Adaptation Plan (rated items/written responses included)

Included a **Turnitin** Originality Report

Included name(s) of group member(s) to indicate who will cover what content

Part Three: Persuasive Presentation Speaking Notes Assessment Form (5 points)

Group Members Names: _____

Topic: _____ **Total Score:** _____ /5

IF YOU SPEAK FROM NOTES OTHER THAN THE ONES SUBMITTED TO YOUR INSTRUCTOR, YOU RISK A SIGNIFICANT DEDUCTION OR A ZERO ON YOUR PRESENTATION DELIVERY SCORE.
(+ = **Excellent** ✔ = **Fair** — = **Poor**)

_____ Speaking notes fit on one 8.5 × 11 page (front only)

_____ Speaking notes are in Times New Roman 12 pt. font (or larger)

_____ Uses proper outline format

_____ Includes introduction in abbreviated form

_____ Includes central idea and initial preview

_____ Includes body section in abbreviated form

_____ Includes supporting material

_____ Includes quotations and pertinent statistical evidence

_____ Includes oral citations

_____ Includes conclusion in abbreviated form

Part Three: Group Persuasive Presentation Assessment Form

Group Members' Names: _____

Topic: _____ **Total Score:** _____/60

_____ **Introduction** (10 points)

Attention
- Gained attention
- Made topic relevant to audience
- Established credibility
- Indicated propositional statement clearly with problem/solution
- Included transition to first point

_____**Body** (30 points)

Need
- Presented problem(s) clearly
- Provided evidence of problem(s)
- Demonstrated relevance of problem(s) with evidence

Satisfaction
- Presented solution(s) clearly
- Proved solution(s) will address problem with evidence

Visualization
- Expressed how implementation of selected solution would impact audience
- Expressed how not implementing selected solution would impact audience

Organization
- Included transitions in the body between main points and points related well
- Cited at least 3 credible sources within problem and solution (1 source in each body paragraph)

_____**Conclusion** (10 points)
- Provided transition from body to conclusion
- Reviewed problem–solution propositional statement

Action
- Provided memorable closure to speech
- Motivated the audience to thought/action

_____**Delivery** (10 points)

_ Used vocal variety and enthusiasm	_ Used notes
_ Used appropriate articulation/pronunciation	_ Used proper speaking rate
_ Established eye contact with audience (no reading)	_ Used precise and clear language
_ Used appropriate gestures and body movement	_ Used minimal vocal disfluencies
_ Team members contributed equally during presentation	_ Fluid transitions between speakers

_____**Met Time Limits** (up to -5)

Part Two: Sample Dewey's Problem-Solving Process Report

Group Members' Names: Taela Fox, Natalie Cavazos, James Doran, Shanna Schultz, & Caroline Waldbeusser.

Instructions: As a group, you will answer each of the questions on this worksheet. Be sure to include full sentences in this report and cite at least three sources (at least one in steps 1, 2, and 5). This will be worth 40 points.

STEP ONE: IDENTIFY AND DEFINE THE PROBLEM

1. *What is the specific problem that concerns us?*

There is not enough on-campus parking available for students at Texas State ("Texas State Transportation Survey of Students", 2011).

2. *What do we want more or less of?*

We would like fewer students who live on campus to be able to park on campus, specifically freshman (since they already live on campus and can walk to class) and more spots available for people who have to drive to campus.

3. *What terms, concepts, or ideas do we need to define in order to understand the problem?*

On-campus parking includes spots available immediately around campus that do not require you to take the bus (this excludes Bobcat Village and Strahan Parking lots).

Types of parking passes sold at Texas State include Red/Restricted Permit, Reserved Red/Restricted, Residence Hall, Mill Street/Residence Hall Permit, Bobcat Village, Commuter/Perimeter Permit, Motorcycle, Reduced Motorcycle, and Texas State Vehicles Including Golf Carts (Student Parking, 2014).

4. *Who is harmed by the problem?*

All students who drive cars and park at Texas State are harmed by the lack of available parking.

STEP TWO: ANALYZE THE PROBLEM

1. *How long has the problem been in existence?*

According to the Texas State Master Plan, parking was a major complaint in 2003. Speaking to older students and professors leads us to believe that it was a significant problem even decades before that.

2. *How widespread is the problem?*

This problem affects all students, faculty, staff, and guests who would like to park on campus at Texas State.

3. *What are the causes of the problem?*

There is not enough parking on campus and there is not enough money in the Parking Budget for Texas State to purchase more land to implement more parking spots ("Student Government Senate Agenda", 2014). Furthermore, university enrollment is expanding and without money in the budget to buy more space, any additional parking growth in the future is limited.

4. *What are the effects of the problem?*

Due to the lack of parking availability at Texas State, students are missing or late for class ("Texas State Transportation Survey of Students", 2011).

5. *What methods already exist for managing the problem?*

In order to accommodate for the lack of parking on campus, the university has a shuttle service that operates on all class days between 7 a.m. and 10:20 p.m. Monday–Thursday and Friday service runs between 7 a.m. and 5 p.m. ("Transportation Services Bobcat Shuttle", 2014). In addition, Transportation Services Advisory Council members reassigned nearly 100 spaces back to all-zone after the tennis courts lot became restricted last semester (Shine, n.d.).

6. *What are the limitations of existing methods?*

The busses are frequently full or there are not enough of them running per route; thus, students are still late or miss class as a result ("Texas State Transportation Survey of Students", 2011). Although the extra spots helped a little, the problem is still significant, and the spots that were rezoned are far away from a lot of the buildings on campus.

7. *What obstacles keep the group from achieving the goal? (Forcefield Analysis)*

Driving forces that favor change to increase the availability of parking spots on campus at Texas State include the overwhelming number of students, staff, and faculty at Texas State who struggle to find parking. In addition, the student government and Nancy Nusbaum, interim director of Transportation Services, have identified this problem and are already working toward change (Jeanes, n.d.). Moreso, students would be more inclined to buy parking passes if they felt that they would be able to find a space near campus ("Texas State Transportation Survey of Students", 2011). On the contrary, restraining forces include the lack of budget money for parking at Texas State ("Student Government Senate Agenda", 2014). Furthermore, the growing number of students being admitted to the university increases the need for more parking. Finally, freshmen are most likely going to be against the idea of them not being allowed to have a car on campus.

8. *What are the criteria we have agreed upon?*
- The solution needs to be inexpensive because of the university's lack in budget money for parking.
- The solution should be agreed upon by the majority.
- The solution should be agreed upon by all group members.
- The solution should be implemented by the fall 2016 semester.

STEP THREE: GENERATE CREATIVE SOLUTIONS

1. *What method did we use to create our solution ideas?*

As a group we used silent brainstorming to come up with a list of creative solutions.

2. *What rules did we adhere to during our brainstorming process?*

During brainstorming we made sure to generate our original ideas on paper first, making sure we thought of as many as possible. Once we had our individual lists, the rules we followed when reading ideas included not evaluating or criticizing the ideas until after everyone shared theirs, piggybacking off of one another's ideas, and making a note when someone had a really wild idea. Also, we also made sure to write down everyone's ideas on a poster board so that we could all visually see them.

3. *What are three solution ideas we have generated?*

Three solutions that we generated included adding on to the existing parking garages, adding more busses, and implementing a no car policy for students who live in the dorms.

STEP FOUR: SELECT THE BEST SOLUTION

1. *How did we evaluate the solution ideas we came up with?*

First, we went through the list and eliminated the ideas that did not meet our criteria and then rated the ones left that we thought best met our goal of having more available on-campus parking spots for people who have to drive to campus.

2. *Which method did we use for selecting the best solution?*

After we rated the remaining solutions, we took a vote as to what we thought were the best solutions. After voting we decided on the solution that the entire group came to a consensus on.

3. *What communication strategies did we use during the evaluation process?*

During our evaluation process, we used a lot of active listening and assigned a devil's advocate to make sure we thought about all the ideas from every perspective and didn't fall victim to groupthink.

4. *What is the final and best solution we decided on?*

The best solution that we chose is to implement a no-car policy for students who live in the residence halls. This means that all students who live in the residence halls will no longer be allowed to have a car on campus (since they can walk everywhere), thus providing more parking spots for people who have to drive to campus.

STEP FIVE: TAKE ACTION

1. *How do we know the solution will solve the problem?*

There are approximately 6,500 students living on campus, most of whom have cars ("Residence Life", 2014). This means that there will be somewhere near that number of available parking spaces open for people who do not live on campus and must drive in, thus increasing the number of available parking spaces on campus. In addition, other universities have already implemented this policy and found that it has helped with the lack of parking, such as Stanford, Pitzer College, and Pomona College (Stanford University Parking and Transportation Services, 2014, & Nemani, 2009).

2. *What are the implications of selecting the proposed solution?*

Consequences include the risk of upsetting students who live on campus and want to have a car with them. Furthermore, this policy has the potential for lowering enrollment rates because of prospective students deciding not to attend Texas State because of the policy; however, in reality, this would probably be a very small percentage.

3. *What are the implications of NOT selecting your other solution ideas?*

The consequence of not adding on to the existing parking garages or adding more busses is that parking could still become an issue if the enrollment rate of transfer students increases.

References

Bradshaw, K. (2014, January 30). Officials propose changes to parking system to alleviate all-zone congestion. *The University Star*. Retrieved from http://star.txstate.edu/node/1422

Campus master plan (2003). Texas State University. Retrieved from http://www.fss.txstate.edu/cmp/process/observations/meetings/obshomecoming. html

Jeanes, R. (n.d.). Officials deserve commendation for parking efforts. *The University Star*. Retrieved from http://star.txstate.edu/node/1431

Nemani, A. (2009, July 5). No cars for freshmen. *The Forum*. Retrieved from http://cmcforum.com/news/07052009-no-cars-for-freshmen

Residence life. (2014). Texas State University Department of Housing and Residential Life. Retrieved from file:///C:/Users/tf1134/Downloads/RESIDENCE%20LIFE%20(1).pdf

Shine, L. (n.d.) Rezoning begins to solve parking problems, more work still needed. *The University Star*. Retrieved from https://star.txstate.edu/node/340/backlinks

Stanford University Parking and Transportation Services. (2014). Stanford University. Retrieved from http://transportation.stanford.edu/parking_info/Resident Student.shtml

Student Government Senate agenda. (2014) Texas State University. Retrieved from http://gato-docs.its.txstate.edu/associated-student-government/Records/Young-Quinones-2014-2015/Minutes-2014-2015/Minutes-9-8-14/Minutes%209.8.14. pdf

Student parking. (2014). Texas State University. Retreived from http://www.parking.txstate.edu/Parking-Information/Student.html

Texas State Transportation Survey of Students. (2011). Texas State University. Retrieved from http://www.fss.txstate.edu/cmp-update/symposia/content Paragraph/0111/document/

Transportation-Survey-Results-Students.pdf"Transportation Services Bobcat Shuttle. (2014). Texas State University. Retrieved from http://www.shuttle.txstate.edu

Parking Made Positive: Sample Preparation Outline

Topic: Lack of Parking at Texas State

I. INTRODUCTION

A. **Attention Getter:**   By a show of hands, who in here is frustrated with the lack of parking at Texas State?

B. **Relevance:**   As most of you are probably aware, there is not enough parking on campus to accommodate all of the people who drive to campus each day. As a student of Texas State, this issue affects you directly and will continue to personally affect you until you no longer are a student at this university.

C. **Credibility:**   We have had to deal firsthand with not being able to find parking as students. Because of this, we have been researching possible solutions and analyzing the situation for weeks.

D. **Propositional Statement:**   Because there are not enough on-campus parking spots available for students who drive to campus at Texas State, we propose that the university implement a no-car policy for students who live on campus.

Transition Statement: Before we can see how this solution will work, we first need to understand the problem and recognize the need for more available parking on campus.

II. BODY

A. Need: There is simply not enough available on-campus parking for the number of students who drive to campus ("Texas State Transportation Survey of Students", 2011).

   1. There is not enough money in the Parking Budget for Texas State to purchase more land to implement more parking spots ("Student Government Senate Agenda", 2014).
      a. Furthermore, the university enrollment is expanding and without money in the budget to buy more space, any additional parking growth in the future is limited.
   2. Many students will not buy parking passes because they know it will be a struggle to find a spot that is anywhere near campus ("Texas State Transportation Survey of Students", 2011).
   3. Students are frequently late to class or miss class because of parking issues ("Texas State Transportation Survey of Students", 2011).

Transition Statement: Undoubtedly, on-campus parking availability is a problem here at Texas State. Luckily, there is a solution.

B. Satisfaction: The best solution is to implement a no-car policy for students who live in the residence halls.

   1. This means that all students who live in the residence halls will no longer be allowed to have a car on campus (since they can walk everywhere), thus providing more parking spots for people who have to drive to campus.
   2. There are approximately 6,500 students living on campus, most of whom have cars ("Residence Life", 2014).
      a. This means that there will be somewhere near that number of available parking spaces open for people who do not live on campus and must drive in, thus increasing the number of available parking spaces on campus.
   3. In addition, other universities have already implemented this policy and found that it has helped with the lack of parking, such as Stanford, Pitzer College, and Pomona College (Stanford University Parking and Transportation Services, 2014, & Nemani, 2009).

Transition Statement: Now that we have a firm understanding of the problem and the proposed solution, let's visualize what your futures will look like if this policy is implemented.

C. Visualization: As students of Texas State, this solution will inevitably affect each and every one of you.

   1. Considering there are approximately 6,500 students living on campus, there is a good chance that some of you do ("Residence Life", 2014). As a resident, this means that you would no longer be able to have a car on campus.

      a. However, this increases the odds that you will be more involved in on-campus activities and spend more time studying (Nemani, 2009).

      b. Additionally, think of the money you will save by not buying gas and a parking permit!

   2. For those of you who live off campus, by implementing this solution you will have more spots available on campus to park when you drive in.

      a. Therefore, you won't have to worry about being late to class or even missing class due to parking.

      b. On the contrary, if the no-car policy is not implemented, negative consequences will continue to manifest.

      c. Students who live on campus will have still have to pay $115 to $485 for a parking pass, on top of gas fees (Student Parking, 2014).

      d. As for the students who live off campus, you will continue to battle to find a parking spot, risk being late to class, and possibly spend $115 for a parking pass that still requires you to park far away and ride a bus (Student Parking, 2014).

Transition Statement: In conclusion …

III. CONCLUSION

A. Problem/Solution Propositional Statement: It is quite evident that there are not enough on-campus parking spots available for students who drive to campus. Due to this, Texas State needs to implement a no-car policy for students who live on campus, thus opening up more spots for people who have to drive in.

B. Memorable Closing: Can you imagine driving to campus and finding a spot within minutes? Can you visualize what it would be like to never be late for class because you couldn't find parking? Fortunately, these dreams can be a reality.

C. Call to Action: To help us make this dream come true, please sign this petition that we have written up to implement this no-car policy and come to school one day without having to worry about parking.

References

Nemani, A. (2009, July 5). No cars for freshmen. *The Forum.* Retrieved from http://cmcforum.com/news/07052009-no-cars-for-freshmen

Residence life. (2014). Texas State University Department of Housing and Residential Life. Retrieved from file:///C:/Users/tf1134/Downloads/RESIDENCE%20LIFE%20(1).pdf

Stanford University Parking and Transportation Services. (2014). Stanford University. Retrieved from http://transportation.stanford.edu/parking_info/ResidentStudent.shtml

Student Government Senate agenda. (2014) Texas State University. Retrieved from http://gato-docs.its.txstate.edu/associated-student-government/Records/Young-Quinones-2014-2015/Minutes-2014-2015/Minutes-9-8-14/Minutes%209.8.14. pdf

Student parking. (2014). Texas State University. Retrieved from http://www.parking.txstate.edu/Parking-Information/Student.html

Texas State Transportation Survey of Students. (2011). Texas State University. Retrieved from http://www.fss.txstate.edu/cmp-update/symposia/contentParagraph/0111/document/Transportation-Survey-Results-Students.pdf

Sample Dewey's Problem-Solving Process Report

Group Members' Names: _____

Instructions: As a group, you will answer each of the questions on this worksheet. Be sure to include full sentences in this report and cite at least three sources (at least one in steps 1, 2, and 5). This will be worth 40 points.

STEP ONE: IDENTIFY AND DEFINE THE PROBLEM

1. *What is the specific problem that concerns us?*
The specific problem that concerns us is the widespread sexually transmitted infection known as herpes or "Bobcat Bumps" at Texas State University (McGarrell, 2013). People who binge drink and people under the influence are three times more likely to contract an STI (American College Help Association, 2009).

2. *What do we want more or less of?*
We would like more students to be aware of the STI herpes and how it can be prevented and reduced at Texas State University.

3. *What terms, concepts, or ideas do we need to define in order to understand the problem?*
The following terms would need to be defined:

- Herpes: a sexually transmitted infection affecting the mouth and/or genitals (FAQ: Herpes, n.d.).
- Brown bag special: a program through the Texas State Health Center that offers condoms for purchase in discreet, brown bags for a reduced price (Services, n.d.).
- Protection: a condom used during intercourse to decrease the risk of infection.
- Abstinence: abstaining completely from sexual intercourse.
- "Safe sex": sexual intercourse in which protection is used.

4. *Who is harmed by the problem?*
Students at Texas State University who are engaging in sexual activity are harmed by this problem.

STEP TWO: ANALYZE THE PROBLEM

1. *How long has the problem been in existence?*
STIs, specifically herpes, have been on the rise in the United States since the 1960s (Aral, Fenton, & Holmes, 2007).

2. *How widespread is the problem?*
The problem affects all those who are sexually active. Typically 1 in 4 students are sexually active and can be infected with the virus while having unprotected sex (10 Truly Shocking, 2010).

3. *What are the causes of the problem?*
Unprotected sex with multiple sexual partners can cause herpes. Alcohol plays a role in influencing decisions about sexual intercourse among college students.

4. *What are the effects of the problem?*
Effects change based on each time you get it. Symptoms can include painful ulcers in the mouth or on the genitals, fever, body aches, swollen lymph nodes, and headaches (Centers for Disease Control and Prevention, 2014).

5. *What methods already exist for managing the problem?*
Although herpes is incurable, it is manageable. It is something you must live with for the rest of your life, and you will continually get outbreaks. There is an antiviral treatment for herpes that can help reduce the likelihood of transmission to another sexual partner (Centers for Disease Control and Prevention, 2014). Herpes cannot be contracted unless the individual is having an outbreak.

6. *What are the limitations of existing methods?*
   Herpes is incurable, so once you have it you will continue to have it for the rest of your life. However, if you educate society on how to prevent it, then you can prevent one more person from conducting it.

7. *What obstacles keep the group from achieving the goal? (Forcefield Analysis)*
   It's expensive to make appointments and get medication. It's time consuming, and not everyone is in a sober state of mind when consenting to sexual activities.

8. *What are the criteria we have agreed upon?*

   • The solution should be sensible and efficient.
   • The solution should be available to everyone.
   • The solution needs to be implemented as soon as possible.

STEP THREE: GENERATE CREATIVE SOLUTIONS

1. *What method did we use to create our solution ideas?*
   The group talked about the issue and researched information about various solutions to this problem. We used general knowledge to come up with multiple solutions. We used the Dewey problem-solving process.

2. *What rules did we adhere to during our brainstorming process?*
   We silently listened to each other's ideas and appropriately joined in on conversations. We each contributed to ideas. Power was distributed evenly, and there was no conflict between one another.

3. *What are three solution ideas we have generated?*
   Three solutions we came up with were abstinence, contraceptives, and sexual awareness.

STEP FOUR: SELECT THE BEST SOLUTION

1. *How did we evaluate the solution ideas we came up with?*
   We researched the infection and used steps 2, 3, and 4 in the John Dewey process. We generated solutions and selected the best solution using the criteria that we agreed upon as a group.

2. *Which method did we use for selecting the best solution?*
   We collectively shared ideas and then discussed which solutions would be most effective and affordable among college students.

3. *What communication strategies did we use during the evaluation process?*
   We used active listening, culture relevance, and a positive sense of power in the evaluation process. The reinforcement stage was used as well.

4. *What is the final and best solution we decided on?*
   College students are unlikely to be abstinent, so we decided to inform our audience on how to effectively prevent the spread of herpes through the use of contraceptives, in hopes they will take action against the disease. We also hope to raise awareness about the importance of making wise choices about alcohol and binge drinking, which often lead to risky sexual decisions.

STEP FIVE: TAKE ACTION

1. *How do we know the solution will solve the problem?*
   Several articles have stated that the use of condoms has been effective and has reduced the spread of herpes by simply protecting one another ("Services," n.d.).

2. *What are the consequences of selecting the proposed solution?*
   Informing students about using condoms may discourage some people from choosing abstinence. However, it is unlikely that the majority of students will choose this; therefore, it is vital to inform them about the importance of safe sex.

3. *What are the consequences of NOT selecting your other solution ideas?*
The consequences of not choosing abstinence is that you don't have a 100% guarantee that you will not get herpes. Abstinence is the only method to be absolutely sure that you will not get an STI.

References

10 truly shocking stats on STDs and college students. (2010). *Nursing Schools.* Retrieved from http://www.nursingschools.net/blog/2010/05/10-truly-shocking-stats-on-stds-and-college-students/

Aral, S. O., Fenton, K. A., & Holmes, K. K. (2007). Sexually transmitted diseases in the USA: Temporal trends. *Sexually Transmitted Infections, 83,* 257–266.

American College Health Association. (2009). Making sex safer. Retrieved from health pamphlet.

FAQ: Herpes. (n.d.). *MIT Medical.* Retrieved from https://medical.mit.edu/faqs/herpes

Centers for Disease Control and Prevention. (2014). *Genital herpes.* Retrieved from http://www.cdc.gov/std/herpes/stdfact-herpes-detailed.htm

McGarrell, I. (2013). STD testing critical for student population. *The University Star.* Retrieved from http://star.txstate.edu/node/1753

Services. (n.d.). *Texas State University Student Health Center.* Retrieved from http://www.healthcenter.txstate.edu/SERVICES/services.html%20

Study Guide for Communicating in Small Group and Team Contexts Module

Chapter 9 Understanding Group and Team Performance

1. Be able to **differentiate** between a group and a team.

2. Be able to **define** and **differentiate** three types of roles within a group: task, social, and individual.

3. Be able to **differentiate** between rules and norms by **identifying** examples of each.

4. Be able to **explain** five types of power: legitimate, referent, expert, reward, and coercive.

5. Be able to **explain** group cohesiveness and its relationship to group productivity.

6. Be able to **recall** Fisher's four phases of group talk: orientation, conflict, emergence, and reinforcement.

Chapter 10 Enhancing Group and Team Performance

1. Be able to **differentiate** structure and interaction within the group process.

2. Be able to **recall** the five steps to John Dewey's reflective thinking process to group problem solving: identify and define the problem, analyze the problem, generate creative solutions, select the best solution, and take action.

3. Be able to **differentiate** traditional brainstorming strategies and the nominal group technique.

4. Be able to **define** groupthink and **identify** key symptoms that characterize groupthink.

5. Be able to **explain** and **differentiate** the trait, functional, styles, situational, and transformational approaches to understanding leadership.

6. Be able to **identify** three steps to managing meeting structure: determine meeting goals, identify what needs to be discussed to achieve the goal, and organize the agenda.

Chapter 13 Delivering Your Presentation

1. Be able to **identify** and **differentiate** four methods of speech delivery: manuscript, memorized, impromptu, and extemporaneous.

2. Be able to **identify** examples of words in a speech that enhance verbal delivery: concrete words, unbiased words, vivid words, simple words, and correct words.

3. Be able to **identify** examples of effective word structures that enhance verbal delivery: figurative language (metaphors, similes, personification), drama (omission, inversion, suspension), and cadence (parallelism, antithesis, repetition, alliteration).

4. Be able to **identify** how the following five components enhance the nonverbal delivery of a presentation: eye contact, physical delivery, facial expressions, vocal delivery, and appearance.

5. Be able to **identify** the 5 Principles of Communication when delivering a presentation.

Chapter 15 Speaking to Persuade

1. Be able to **define** persuasion.

2. Be able to **recall** and **identify** ways to motivate an audience, including motivating with dissonance, motivating with fear appeals, and motivating with positive appeals.

3. Be able to **differentiate** attitudes, beliefs, and values.

4. Be able to **differentiate** propositions of fact, value, and policy.

5. Be able to **define** credibility (ethos) and **differentiate** its factors: competence, trustworthiness, and dynamism/charisma.

6. Be able to **define** proof (logos) and **differentiate** evidence from reasoning.

7. Be able to **identify** the following organizational patterns for persuasive messages: problem and solution, cause and effect, and motivated sequence.

8. Be able to **identify** strategies for persuading receptive, neutral, and unreceptive audiences.

9. Be able to **identify** the 5 Principles of Communication when speaking to persuade.

Sample Exam Questions
Module: Communicating in Small
Group and Team Contexts

Chapter 9 Understanding Group and Team Performance

1. Michael, James, and Cynthia meet every Thursday night to help each other on math problems. They are engaging in what type of communication?

    A. Interpersonal
    B. Dyadic
    C. Public
    D. Small group

2. While trying to plan a new arrangement of the store, H-E-B grocery supermarket gathered random customers to discuss their opinions. The information collected was used to improve the store and make the design more efficient. These individuals formed what type of group?

    A. Focus group
    B. Problem-solving group
    C. Primary group
    D. Social group

3. George has just been elected to serve as class president. Group members give him power because of his title or because of his elected position of authority.

    A. Referent
    B. Expert
    C. Reward
    D. Legitimate

4. The group you belong to on campus is finally making some decisions that group members feel good about. A common point of view has finally emerged from the group, and conflict and disagreement are being managed well. Group problems are also being solved. What phase of group development is your group experiencing?

    A. Orientation
    B. Conflict
    C. Emergence
    D. Reinforcement

5. Which of the following is NOT a similarity that exists between a group and a team:

    A. Both groups and teams have roles, even though they may not be clearly defined.
    B. Both groups and teams have some sort of goal that the members share.
    C. Individuals in both groups and teams influence each other.
    D. Both groups and teams have clear methods of collaborating and coordinating their efforts.

Chapter 10 Enhancing Group and Team Performance

1. The give-and-take discussion in a group and the group members' responsiveness to each other's comments refers to the group's:

    A. Structure
    B. Action
    C. Interaction
    D. Management

2. Russ, the professor for Small Group Communication, first asked students in the class to generate ideas individually before getting into groups. Once the students wrote down their ideas, they were told to get into groups and share their ideas with other group members. This is an example of:

   A. Nominal group technique
   B. Traditional brainstorming
   C. Delphi technique
   D. Consensus technique

3. In order to reach consensus, Jimmy and his group are goal oriented and promote honest dialogue and discussion in the group. What other strategy does the group need to use to reach consensus?

   A. Encourage groupthink
   B. Listen to each other
   C. Ask experts for advice
   D. Talk as much as possible

4. Bob is a member of a group that is trying to solve a problem. Two members of the group have proposed possible solutions to the problem. Rather than analyzing the pros and cons of each solution, the entire group settles on the solution proposed by the leader of the group to avoid conflict. What type of decision-making method has the group used?

   A. Consensus
   B. Groupthink
   C. Expert
   D. Analysis paralysis

5. Justin states to his group, "I do not understand this conversation. Can someone explain how the solution relates to our goal?" Justin's comment reflects:

   A. Gatekeeping
   B. Metadiscussion
   C. Consensus
   D. Brainstorming

Chapter 13   Delivering Your Presentation

1. Gina must give a presentation to her colleagues concerning ethics in the workplace. She has ample time to prepare, and crafts her speech very carefully according to the various stages of the audience-centered public-speaking model. Before she speaks, she rehearses several times and delivers from an outline. When she presents, she speaks using a few note cards and gives the impression that she is creating the speech for the first time. Her speech is delivered using which style of delivery?

   A. Manuscript
   B. Impromptu
   C. Memorized
   D. Extemporaneous

2. Words that refer to an object or action in the most specific way possible are called:

   A. Unbiased
   B. Vivid
   C. Correct
   D. Concrete

3. Lisa takes one step each time she transitions between main ideas. Her steps are an example of:

   A. Gestures

   B. Posture

   C. Appearance

   D. Movement

4. Jesse makes sure that he clearly enunciates the sounds of each word. What element of vocal delivery is Jesse using?

   A. Volume

   B. Pitch

   C. Articulation

   D. Rate

5. Donald gave a speech to the school board about the need for tougher discipline in high schools. In his speech he started each sentence with the same phrase: "Because of the lack of discipline . . . ." Which of the following forms of language rhythm did Donald use?

   A. Alliteration

   B. Antithesis

   C. Parallelism

   D. Repetition

Chapter 15   Speaking to Persuade

1. Nicholas must give a speech in his communication class. He wants his audience to believe that censorship of music, art, and literature should be put to an end because it is in violation of the First Amendment. He also advocates contacting legislators and engaging in peaceful protest to affect this change. The purpose of his speech will be to:

   A. Entertain

   B. Inform

   C. Persuade

   D. Illustrate

2. The sense of disorganization or imbalance that prompts a person to change when new information conflicts with previously organized thought patterns represents which motivational strategy?

   A. Persuasion

   B. Needs

   C. Fear appeals

   D. Cognitive dissonance

3. A person's sense of what is true or false is a/an:

   A. Attitude

   B. Belief

   C. Value

   D. Predisposition

4. Congress should make more national parks to preserve America's forests." This statement is an example of what type of proposition?

   A. Fact

   B. Value

   C. Policy

   D. Interest

5. A speaker who is perceived as knowledgeable, honest, and energetic is also perceived as:
   A. Credible
   B. Charismatic
   C. Logical
   D. Emotional

Answer Key

CHAPTER 9

1. D
2. A
3. D
4. C
5. D

CHAPTER 10

1. C
2. A
3. B
4. B
5. B

CHAPTER 13

1. D
2. D
3. D
4. C
5. D

CHAPTER 15

1. C
2. D
3. B
4. C
5. A

Comm 1310 Instructor Evaluation Forms

In the following section, you will find several perforated pages for you to remove and complete to provide us with feedback on how we are doing.

Midterm Instructor Evaluation Form

This questionnaire is designed to obtain information that will assist your lab instructor in improving his or her teaching. Your responses are considered very important, and your cooperation is appreciated. Responses can be left anonymous or you may sign your name to your questionnaire.

Please respond to the following statements by circling the number that reflects your level of agreement/disagreement:

1. My Instructor is consistently well prepared for class and class activities.
   Disagree   1   2   3   4   5   6   7   Agree

2. The in-class activities help me understand the communication concepts that we are studying.
   Disagree   1   2   3   4   5   6   7   Agree

3. My Instructor keeps our class focused on our learning objectives.
   Disagree   1   2   3   4   5   6   7   Agree

4. My Instructor demonstrates an understanding of material covered in the course.
   Disagree   1   2   3   4   5   6   7   Agree

5. My Instructor maintains a professional manner.
   Disagree   1   2   3   4   5   6   7   Agree

6. My Instructor can convey the course concepts clearly.
   Disagree   1   2   3   4   5   6   7   Agree

7. My Instructor is enthusiastic about teaching the course.
   Disagree   1   2   3   4   5   6   7   Agree

8. My Instructor is interested in me as an individual.
   Disagree   1   2   3   4   5   6   7   Agree

Please provide a brief answer for the following:

What is the most successful part of your class experience?

What would you like to see changed?

Midterm Lecturer Evaluation Form

Large Section Lecturer: _____

Semester: _____ Day(s) and Time: _____

Evaluate the performance of the large section lecturer using the following scale:

1 = Strongly Disagree   2 = Disagree   3 = Undecided   4 = Agree   5 = Strongly Agree

1. The lecturer is knowledgeable in the subject matter.   1   2   3   4   5

2. The lecturer provides clear objectives for the course.   1   2   3   4   5

3. The lecturer gives lectures that are informative.   1   2   3   4   5

4. The lecturer is enthusiastic.   1   2   3   4   5

5. The lecturer organizes the course well.   1   2   3   4   5

6. The lecturer demonstrates concern for students.   1   2   3   4   5

7. The lecturer gives lectures that are interesting.   1   2   3   4   5

8. The lecturer provides assignments that effectively accomplished the course objectives.   1   2   3   4   5

9. Compared to other lecturers I've had at Texas State, this lecturer is excellent.   1   2   3   4   5

10. I would recommend this lecturer to other students.   1   2   3   4   5

11. What are the strengths of this lecturer?   1   2   3   4   5

12. What are the weaknesses of this lecturer?   1   2   3   4   5

Final Lecturer Evaluation Form

The Purpose of This Course Evaluation:

This questionnaire is designed to obtain information that will assist your instructor in improving his/her teaching as well as to serve as one means for evaluating teaching effectiveness. Your responses are considered very important; we appreciate your cooperation. Your instructor will read this evaluation form after grades are turned in, so your anonymity is guaranteed.

Instructions

USE THE TEXAS STATE ANSWER SHEET AND A PENCIL TO RECORD YOUR RESPONSES. In the section labeled "Your Last Name," write the last name of *your instructor*, but you do not need to darken the letters below your instructor's name. In the section labeled "Course ID," write the course number of this course (for example, 1310), but you do not need to darken the number below. In the section labeled "Sect. #," write the section number of this course, but you do not need to darken the number below. You need NOT identify the "Test Form" or "Student I.D. Number."

For Items 1–18, use the following scale:

A = Strongly Disagree   **B** = Disagree   **C** = Undecided   **D** = Agree   **E** = Strongly Agree

About the Course

1. This course was intellectually challenging and stimulating.

2. This course increased my interest in the subject matter.

3. The syllabus was clear and complete.

4. The objectives and goals of the course were clear.

5. Class sessions were well organized.

6. I like the textbook(s) used in this course.

7. The exams/assignments appropriately covered the concepts in the assigned readings and material covered in class.

8. I learned a great deal in this course.

About the Instructor

9. The instructor was responsive to my questions.

10. The instructor was concerned and interested in students as individuals.

11. The instructor motivated me to do my best work.

12. The instructor was available during his/her scheduled (posted) office hours.

13. The instructor's explanations were clear.

14. The instructor is a well-organized lecturer.

15. The instructor effectively demonstrated his/her knowledge of the course content.

16. The instructor clearly communicated how grades would be determined.

17. The instructor was enthusiastic in presenting course material and appeared to enjoy teaching.

18. Because this instructor employed principles of good teaching, I would recommend him/her to other students.
(Questions continue on reverse side of this sheet.)

19. The course content was difficult, relative to other *required* courses I have taken:
(A) Strongly Disagree   (B) Disagree   (C) Undecided   (D) Agree   (E) Strongly Agree

20. The course workload, relative to other *"required* courses I have taken, was:
(A) Very Light   (B) Light   (C) Average   (D) Heavy   (E) Very Heavy

21. The course pace, relative to other *required* courses I have taken, was:
(A) Very Slow   (B) Slow   (C) Average   (D) Fast   (E) Very Fast

Everyone completing this form, please answer the following questions:

22. I am:
(A) a COMM major   (B) a COMM minor   (C) Not a COMM major or minor

23. I am classified as a:
(A) Freshman   (B) Sophomore   (C) Junior   (D) Senior   (E) Graduate

24. My estimate of my current grade in this course is:
(A) A   (B) B   (C) C   (D) D   (E) F

25. I am a:
(A) Male   B) Female

26. My current Grade Point Average (GPA) is:
(A) less than 2.00   (B) 2.00–2.50   (C) 2.51–3.00   (D) 3.01–3.50   (E) 3.51 or higher

27. This course is:
(A) COMM 1310   (B) COMM 1340 or a 2000-level course
(C) 3000-level course   (D) 4000-level course   (E) 5000-level course

On the reverse side of the green Texas State answer sheet (not on this sheet), please provide answers to items 28, 29, and 30. These open-ended comments will be very useful to your instructor.

28. Things I like best about this course/instructor include:

29. My suggestions for improving this course are:

30. Other comments or suggestions:

Notes

Notes

Notes

Notes

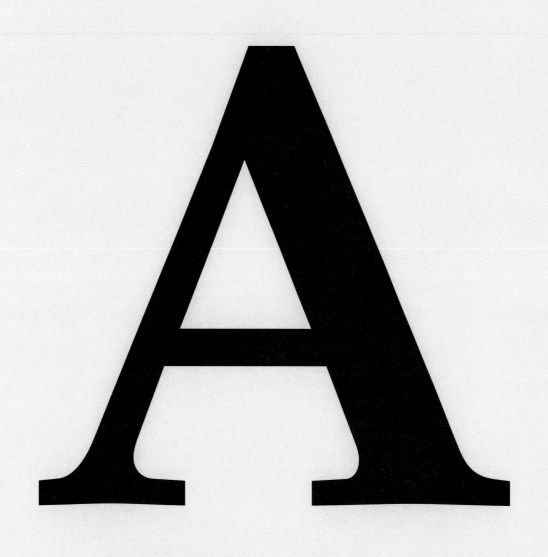

B

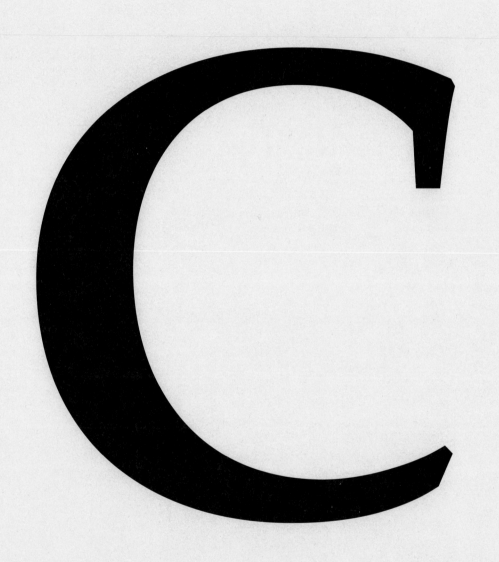

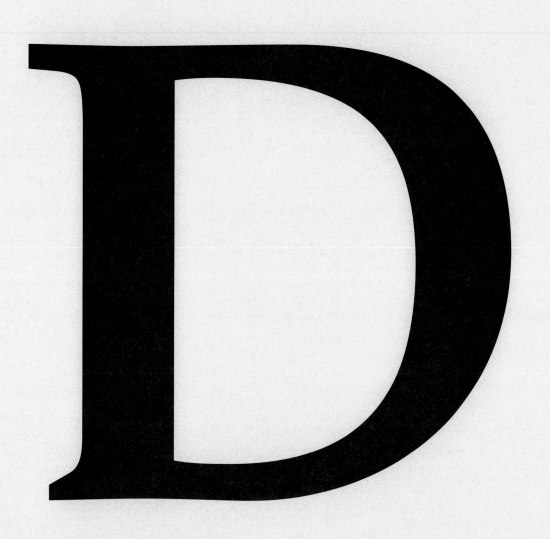

Centennial Hall Teaching Theater

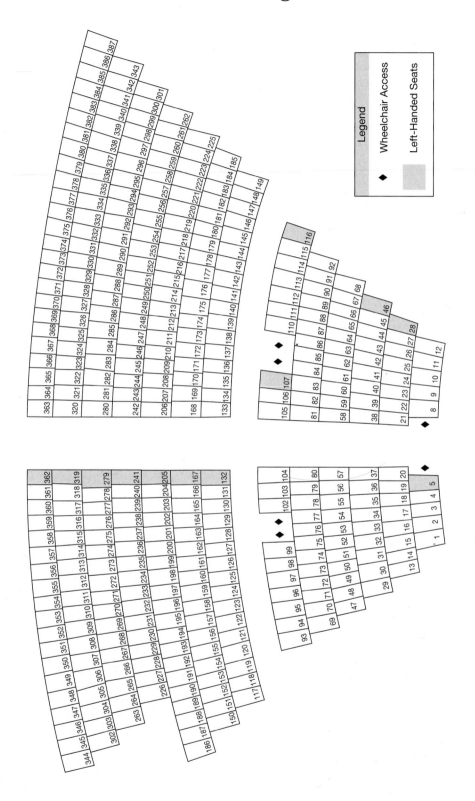